The
Economist
Books

GUIDE TO MANAGEMENT IDEAS

OTHER TITLES FROM
THE ECONOMIST BOOKS

The Economist Desk Companion
The Economist Economics
The Economist Guide to Economic Indicators
The Economist Guide to Financial Markets
The Economist Guide to the European Union
The Economist Numbers Guide
The Economist Style Guide
The Guide to Analysing Companies
The Dictionary of Economics
The International Dictionary of Finance
Going Digital
Improving Marketing Effectiveness
Measuring Business Performance
Management Development

Pocket Accounting
Pocket Advertising
Pocket Director
Pocket Finance
Pocket Information Technology
Pocket International Business Terms
Pocket Investor
Pocket Internet
Pocket Law
Pocket Manager
Pocket Marketing
Pocket MBA
Pocket Negotiator
Pocket Strategy
Pocket Telecommunications

The Economist Pocket Asia
The Economist Pocket Europe in Figures
The Economist Pocket World in Figures

GUIDE TO MANAGEMENT IDEAS

Tim Hindle

THE ECONOMIST IN ASSOCIATION WITH
PROFILE BOOKS LTD

Published by Profile Books Ltd
58A Hatton Garden, London ECIN 8LX

Text copyright © Tim Hindle, 2000
Copyright © The Economist Newspaper Ltd, 2000

The greatest care has been taken in compiling this book.
However, no responsibility can be accepted by the publishers or compilers
for the accuracy of the information presented.

Where opinion is expressed it is that of the author and does not necessarily coincide
with the editorial views of The Economist Newspaper.

Typeset in EcoType by MacGuru
macguru2@appleonline.net

Printed in Great Britain by
St Edmundsbury Press, Bury St Edmunds

A CIP catalogue record for this book is available
from the British Library

ISBN 1 86197 154 0

Contents

Introduction

This book was written largely because I felt a need for it. I could find no single volume that contained short introductions to the main management concepts that have determined the structure and style of business organisations over the last century. These concepts are no longer confined to the pages of learned management journals or to the lecture halls of prestigious business schools. Many of them are increasingly referred to in general-management training material and in the pages of the everyday business press. Yet few of them are self-explanatory.

Without a book like this, it seems to me, studying business and management is a bit like viewing an art gallery without knowing anything about the artists: it can be rewarding, but for any long-term appreciation you are much better off with a guide.

This particular guide is designed to lead the interested reader on to further learning through the list of recommended reading that concludes the majority of the entries. My original aim was to compile the 100 greatest management ideas of the 20th century, an average of one big idea per year being about as much as anyone could hope for. Although this is not the title of the book, it could well have been. For it does contain exactly 100 "ideas".

Most of them selected themselves. But a minority could as easily have been replaced by others, the choice being ultimately a matter of opinion. In this case, my opinion guided by that of Professor Piero Morosini of IMD, a business school in Lausanne. But, as always with such a compilation, any serious omissions are my fault, and for them I apologise.

As I progressed with the book I became more and more amazed by the range and depth of ideas on the subject of the organisation and behaviour of "people at work", of human beings as producers and consumers. I was also struck by the cyclical nature of so many of them. They come and they go, and then they come back again. The similarities between Frederick Taylor's scientific management and the late 20th-century enthusiasm for business process re-engineering are striking. So too is the frequent resurrection of Douglas McGregor's Theories X and Y, and the currently neglected insight in the idea of satisficing, long due for a revival if only to be applied to the world of e-commerce.

I would like to thank Stephen Brough at Profile Books for believing with me that there was a market other than myself for a product like this. Thanks also to Aimee-Jane Lee of Worcester College, Oxford, for her tremendous help in researching many of the entries, and to Piero Morosini, who gave time and effort both to encourage me and to keep me on the intellectual straight and narrow.

Lastly, I would like to thank all the management thinkers and writers referred to in the book. Unfortunately, many of them have suffered from the volumes of management mumbo-jumbo that are published every year and give the genre a bad name. But the best of them throw extraordinary flashes of insight on to the way that most of us spend the greater part of our waking day. If this book mirrors just a few of those flashes it will have achieved its aim.

Tim Hindle
January 2000

Activity-based costing

Activity-based costing (ABC) is a system of assigning costs to products or services based on the resources that they consume. Its aim, says *The Economist*, is "to change the way in which costs are counted".

ABC is an alternative to the traditional way of accounting in which a business's overheads (indirect costs such as lighting, heating and marketing) are allocated in proportion to an activity's direct costs. This is unsatisfactory because two activities that absorb the same direct costs can use different amounts of overhead. A mass-produced industrial robot, for instance, may use the same amount of labour and materials as a customised robot. But the customised robot uses far more of the company engineers' time (an overhead) than does the mass-produced one.

This difference would not be reflected in traditional costing systems. Hence a company that makes more and more customised products (and bases its pricing on historic costings) can soon find itself making large losses. As new technologies make it easier for firms to customise products, the importance of allocating indirect costs accurately increases.

Introducing activity-based costing is not a simple task – it is by no means as easy as ABC. For a start, all business activities must be broken down into their discrete components. As part of its ABC programme, for example, ABB, a Swiss-Swedish power company, divided its purchasing activity into things like negotiating with suppliers, updating the database, issuing purchase orders and handling complaints.

Large firms should try a pilot scheme before implementing the system throughout their organisation. The information essential for ABC is often not readily available and has to be calculated specially for the purpose. This involves making many new measurements. Bigger companies usually hire consultants who are specialists in the area to help them get a system up and running properly.

The easy approach is to use ABC software in conjunction with a company's existing accounting system. The traditional system continues to be used as before, and the ABC structure is an extra to be called upon when specific cost information is required to help make a decision. The development of new business accounting software programs, such as those of SAP, a German software company, have made the introduction of activity-based costing more feasible.

Setting up an activity-based costing system is a prerequisite for

1

improving business processes (see page 179) and for any re-engineering programme (see page 186). Many firms also use ABC data as inputs for the measures required for a balanced scorecard (see page 3).

A brief history

The idea of activity-based costing arose in the early 1980s as a result of growing dissatisfaction with traditional ways of allocating costs. The idea owes much to the work of Michael Porter (see Competitive advantage, page 35), who developed the view of the business as a chain of interlinked activities. In his scheme, profits are no more than the sum of the difference between the price that customers pay for an activity and the cost of that activity. Measuring the cost of activities correctly then becomes central to making a profit.

After a strong start, however, ABC fell into a period of disrepute. Even Robert Kaplan, a Harvard Business School professor sometimes credited with being its founding father, has admitted that it stagnated in the 1990s. The difficulty lay in translating the theory into action. Many companies were not prepared to give up their traditional cost-control mechanisms in favour of ABC. In his book Cost & Effect, Kaplan claims that "most users are taking advantage of only a fraction of the potential benefits of modern cost management".

Nevertheless, ABC has many satisfied customers. Chrysler, an American automobile manufacturer now merged with Daimler-Benz, claims that it saved hundreds of millions of dollars through a programme that it introduced in the early 1990s. ABC showed that the true cost of certain Chrysler parts was 30 times what had originally been estimated, a discovery that led the company to outsource (see page 163) the manufacture of many of those parts.

Recommended reading

Kaplan, R., and Cooper, R., "Make Cost Right: Make the Right Decisions", Harvard Business Review, September-October 1988

Kaplan, R., Cost & Effect, Harvard Business School Press, 1997

Ness, J.A. and Cucuzza, T.G., "Tapping the Full Potential of ABC", Harvard Business Review, July-August 1995

O'Guin, M.C., The Complete Guide to Activity Based Costing, Prentice Hall, 1991

www.dtic.mil/c3i/bprcd/0201c1.htm – ABC Guidebook

Balanced scorecard

Robert Kaplan, a professor of accounting at Harvard Business School, is a man who comes up with one big idea per decade. In the 1980s it was activity-based costing (see page 1); in the 1990s it was the balanced scorecard.

The idea of the balanced scorecard is set out in an article that Kaplan wrote in 1992 for the *Harvard Business Review*, along with David Norton, president of a consulting firm called Renaissance Strategy Group. The article, entitled "The Balanced Scorecard – Measures that Drive Performance", began with the idea that what you measure is what you get. If you measure only financial performance, then you get only financial performance. If you take a wider view, and measure things from different perspectives as well, then (and only then) do you stand a chance of achieving goals other than purely financial ones.

In particular, Kaplan and Norton suggested that companies should consider the following.

- **The customer's perspective.** How does the customer see the organisation, and what does the organisation need to do in order to remain that customer's valued supplier?
- **The company's internal perspective.** What are the internal processes that the company must improve if it is to achieve its objectives vis-à-vis customers, shareholders and others.
- **Innovation and improvement.** How can the company continue to improve and to create value in the future? What should it be measuring to make this happen?

A brief history

The idea of the balanced scorecard was highly attractive when it first appeared. Companies were increasingly frustrated with traditional measures of performance that related only to the shareholders' point of view. Many felt that this was unduly short-termist and obsessively concerned with stockmarket twitches, and that it prevented boardrooms and managers from considering longer-term opportunities. The balanced scorecard not only broadened the organisation's perception of where it stood today, but also helped it to identify things that would ensure its success in the future.

Kaplan and Norton themselves saw some of the benefits of the balanced scorecard as follows.

- It helps companies to focus on what has to be done in order to create a "breakthrough performance".
- It acts as an integrating device for a variety of often disconnected corporate programmes, such as quality, re-engineering, process redesign and customer service.
- It makes strategy operational by translating it into performance measures and targets.
- It helps to break down corporate-level measures so that local managers and employees can see what they need to do well if they want to improve organisational effectiveness.
- It provides a comprehensive view that overturns the traditional idea of the organisation as a collection of isolated, independent functions and departments.

Recommended reading

Kaplan, R.S. and Norton, D.P., "The Balanced Scorecard – Measures that Drive Performance", *Harvard Business Review*, January-February 1992

Kaplan, R.S. and Norton, D.P., "Putting the Balanced Scorecard to Work", *Harvard Business Review*, September-October 1993

Kaplan, R.S. and Norton, D.P., *The Balanced Scorecard: Translating Strategy into Action*, Harvard Business School Press, 1996

Kaplan, R.S. and Norton, D.P., "Why Does Business Need a Balanced Scorecard?", *Journal of Strategic Performance Measurement*, Part 1, February-March 1997; Part 2, June-July 1997

Neely, A., *Measuring Business Performance*, Profile Books, 1998

Barriers to entry, exit and mobility

The idea that there are barriers preventing firms from entering markets and barriers preventing them from leaving those markets is taken from economics. Markets are viewed as being similar to fields surrounded by gates of differing sizes and complexity. The gates have to be surmounted by firms wishing to enter or leave these markets.

To some extent the gates can be both raised and lowered, not just by those inside the fields but also by those outside wishing to enter. Typical barriers to entry include patents, licensing agreements and exclusive access to natural resources. A patented pharmaceutical, for instance, gives the patent holder exclusive rights for a certain period (usually a maximum of seven years) to manufacture and sell that pharmaceutical within a specified market.

The economies of scale (see page 76) that can be gained from being large and established in a particular field can also act as a barrier to entry. If new entrants calculate that they need to sell large volumes before they can hope to be competitive with existing firms, this acts as a deterrent to their ambition. When, for instance, did a new entrant last try to begin manufacturing for the mass car market?

Barriers to entry can also be erected by governments. Regulations covering the financial services industry are designed to act as a barrier to rogues and villains, but inevitably they also deter many honest businesses too. Until recently, foreign banks could not operate in the UK unless they had an office within walking distance of the Bank of England, then the industry's regulator. Needless to say, property prices in the City of London's "Square Mile" were among the highest in the world and acted as a powerful barrier to entry into the City.

Firms that are well established in a particular field or market may be tempted to increase the barriers when they see a newcomer approaching their patch. They can do this, for instance, by lowering their prices, thus making the newcomers' products less competitive. Moreover, lowering prices may be an easy option for the incumbents since their prices may well be higher than the free-market level because of the barriers.

Monopolies exist where there are insurmountable barriers to entry. If there were no (or only low) barriers, other firms would enter monopoly markets to participate in the monopoly profits. They would then, by definition, no longer be monopoly markets.

Barriers to exit make it harder for a company to get out of a particular business than it would otherwise have been. They include things like the cost of laying off staff and contractual obligations, such as the payment of rent. For a classic high-street bank with a large number of staff and a wide network of branches, the barriers to exit from traditional banking businesses are considerable.

Paradoxically, firms sometimes decide for themselves to erect barriers that hinder their own exit from a market. This can be a strategic ploy designed to convey to their competitors the message that they are committed to that market, and that they are not going to leave it in a hurry.

Barriers to mobility are the gates that hinder a firm from one industry from moving into another (or, as Michael Porter put it in *Competitive Strategy*, first published in 1980, "factors that deter the movement of firms from one strategic position to another"). For example, supermarkets in the UK that wish to go into the banking business are prevented from doing so on their own. They have to form an alliance with an existing registered bank because UK regulators do not yet countenance the selling of loans and of soap powder by the same organisation. Similarly, supermarkets face huge barriers to becoming online Internet service providers, not least of which is the fact that they own massive chunks of land and buildings.

A brief history

Old ideas about barriers to entry were given a new twist with the development of electronic commerce (e-commerce, see page 74). By using the Internet, firms can sometimes surmount traditional barriers with an ease not previously available. Economies of scale, for instance, do not apply in the same way in the world of e-commerce.

The wave of deregulation in the 1980s and 1990s was designed by free-market-oriented governments to lower barriers to entry in industries ranging from airlines to stockbroking. But it had only limited success. A 1996 study of the airline industry by the US government's General Accounting Office, for example, illustrated the complex way in which barriers to entry become woven into the fabric of an industry. The study found that:

- three things – namely, limits on take-off and landing slots at certain major airports; the existence of long-term leases giving airlines the exclusive use of airport gates; and rules prohibiting flights of less than a certain distance – continued to impede new airlines' access to airports;

◪ established airlines' marketing strategies – such as travel agents' commissions, frequent-flier plans, airline-owned computer reservation systems and partnerships with commuter airlines – made it extremely difficult for other carriers to attract traffic.

Recommended reading

Geroski, P., Gilbert, R. and Jacquemin, A., "Barriers to Entry and Strategic Competition (Fundamentals of Pure and Applied Economics; Theory of the Firm and Industrial Organization, Vol. 41)", Harwood Academic Publishers, 1990

Karakaya, F. and Stahl, M.J., *Entry Barriers and Market Entry Decisions*, Greenwood Publishing Group, 1991

Porter, M., *Competitive Strategy*, The Free Press, 1980

Benchmarking

Benchmarking is a way of determining how well a business unit or organisation is performing in comparison to other units elsewhere. It sets a business's measures of its own performance in a broad context and gives it an idea of what is best practice. In *The Benchmarking Book*, Michael Spendolini defines benchmarking as a "continuous systematic process for evaluating the products, services or work processes of organisations that are recognised as representing the best practices for the purposes of organisational improvement".

Historically, measures of corporate performance were compared with previous measures from the same organisation at different times. Although this gave a good indication of the rate of improvement within the organisation, it gave no indication of where the performance stood in absolute terms. The organisation could be getting better and better; but if its competitors were improving even more, then better and better was not enough.

In their book, *Benchmarking, a Tool for Continuous Improvement*, C.J. McNair and H.J. Liebfried describe four different types of benchmarking.

1 **Internal benchmarking.** This is a bit like the process of quality management, an internal checking of the organisation's standards to see if there is further potential to cut waste and improve efficiency.
2 **Competitive benchmarking.** This is the comparison of one company's standards with those of another (rival) company.
3 **Industry benchmarking.** Here the comparison is between a company's standards and those of the industry to which it belongs.
4 **Best-in-class benchmarking.** This is a comparison of a company's level of achievement with the best anywhere in the world, regardless of industry or national market. The Japanese have a word for it, *dantotsu*, which means "being the best of the best".

Benchmarking is a fluid concept which recognises that the relative importance of different processes changes over time as the business itself changes. For example, a retailer that shifts from selling through stores to selling over the Internet suddenly becomes less concerned about customer parking facilities and more concerned about the performance of its fleet of delivery vans. The importance of benchmarking these respective activities changes similarly.

The process of benchmarking assumes that companies are prepared to put their measures into some sort of public arena where others can use them for comparison. This is usually carried out by a third party, who puts the data in order and then discloses it in a way that does not reveal the identity of any individual data provider. Firms can recognise their own data and judge where they stand in the pecking order.

A brief history

The enthusiasm for benchmarking grew out of two things.

- The Japanese development of total quality management (see page 225) and the idea of *kaizen* (see page 126), that is, continuous improvement. This was a system built on detailed statistics. It required careful measurement of industrial activities, followed by close monitoring of those measures. It not only forced managers to make such measurements; it made their competitors do so too.
- The work of Michael Porter (see Competitive advantage, page 35) in the 1980s. This forced firms to think more about their competitors and where they stood in relation to them rather than where they stood in terms of their own history.

One of the best-known examples of benchmarking is that of Xerox, a photocopying company which underwent a rigorous benchmarking exercise in the 1980s after it had watched its market share being whittled away by Japanese competition. The company systematically analysed its competitors' products and their production processes with the aim of reorganising itself, not just to match the opposition but to exceed it. By 1989 Xerox had regained much of its market share and that year won the prestigious Malcolm Baldrige Quality Award in the United States.

Benchmarking has become common practice in the United States and Japan, and is increasingly used in Europe. For example, Siemens, a German electrical and electronics firm, has benchmarked itself extensively against its rivals and against firms in other industries (such as retailing) in order to gain a better idea of how it might improve in areas such as customer service.

Recommended reading

Ahlstrom, P., Blacknon, K. and Voss, C., "Benchmarking and Manufacturing Performance: Some Empirical Results", *Business Strategy Review*, Vol. 4, 1996

Boxwell, R.J., *Benchmarking for Competitive Advantage*, McGraw-Hill, 1994

Karlof, B., *The Benchmarking Management Guide*, 1993

McNair, C.J. and Liebfried, H.J., *Benchmarking: A tool for continuous improvement*, John Wiley, 1992

www.pr.doe.gov/dg61-3.html – Special focus area: Benchmarking

Brainstorming

Brainstorming is a rather dramatic name for a semi-structured business meeting whose chief purpose is to come up with new ideas. It is loosely based on belief in a sort of psychological synergy: that a creative meeting can throw out something more than the sum of its parts, that is, more than the sum of the ideas in the participants' heads.

To be most effective, brainstorming sessions require a trained facilitator and some basic ground rules. Without a facilitator, such sessions often degenerate into an effort to find as many negative points as possible about each new idea. Ultimately, the idea is cast aside and the group prepares to give the same treatment to the next one.

Formalised brainstorming contains three basic rules.

1 Participants should be encouraged to come up with as many ideas as possible, however wild they are.
2 No judgment should be passed on any idea until the end of the session.
3 Participants should be encouraged to build on each other's ideas, putting together unlikely combinations and taking each one in unlikely directions.

For those wishing to try out brainstorming, there are a number of generally agreed hints.

- Identify a precise topic to be discussed.
- If there are more than ten participants split the discussion into smaller groups.
- Make each group choose a secretary to record the ideas that are thrown up.
- Explain clearly the three basic rules above.
- Storm away with ideas, with the secretary listing all that come up.
- Establish criteria for selecting the best ideas, then evaluate each idea against these criteria.
- Outline the steps needed to implement these best ideas.

A brief history
Brainstorming is said to have been popularised as a management

technique in the late 1930s by an advertising executive, Alex Osborn. At one time the technique was widely used within corporations to help them come up with new product ideas or to devise radically new manufacturing processes. The results of brainstorming, however, have often been judged to be inadequate. Most people agree that totally unstructured sessions rarely work. But even when basic rules are followed, the results are frequently disappointing.

Research into the effectiveness of brainstorming suggests that individuals working on their own come up with more original and higher-quality ideas. But groups come up with more ideas as such, even though they may be of an inferior quality. Groups also go on being productive for much longer; individuals on their own tire easily and dry up.

Where open-ended group discussions have been found to be particularly helpful is in evaluating ideas rather than in generating them. Group feedback seems to be useful here.

Recommended reading

De Bono, E., *Serious Creativity*, HarperBusiness, 1992
Goman, C.K., *Creative Thinking in Business*, Kogan Page, 1989
Rawlinson, J.G., *Creative Thinking and Brainstorming*, Wildwood House, 1986

Branding

Originally, branding was the placing on animals (usually by burning) of an identifying mark. In a business context, branding refers to imposing on goods and services a distinctive identity. Philip Kotler, author of *Marketing Management*, one of the world's standard textbooks on marketing, defines a brand as: "A name, term, symbol or design (or a combination of them) which is intended to signify the goods or services of one seller or group of sellers and to differentiate them from those of the competitors."

A brand's image is conveyed in a variety of ways, including advertising, packaging and the attitudes of employees. Inevitably, it has to be continually modified to keep up with the cultural times.

Branding bestows a number of benefits on goods and services.

◪ **It reassures consumers about the quality of the product.** This allows the producer to charge a premium over and above the value of the basic benefits provided by the underlying product. Consumers buy Coca-Cola not just because they like the taste, but because when it comes to colas, the Coca-Cola brand name is a well-known "guarantee" of quality.

The ability of powerful brands to grab a bigger share of consumers' wallets than lesser-known competing products can give them great value. When Philip Morris bought the Kraft food company in 1988 it paid four times the value of Kraft's tangible assets. Most of the 75% spent on intangible assets represented the value of Kraft's powerful brands. When Nestlé bought Rowntree it paid more than five times the book value of Rowntree's assets. Most of that extra (almost £2 billion) was the cost of Rowntree's well-known names, such as Polo, Kit-Kat and After Eight.

The confidence that consumers gain from a well-known brand is particularly useful when they do not have enough information to make wise choices about goods and services. Thus western travellers seek out global brand names when buying drinks and cigarettes, for example, in far-flung corners of the earth where they have no knowledge of the local produce.

Another area where this applies is on the Internet, where online shoppers may be uncomfortable with the multitude of choices presented to them. In order to feel they are getting reliable quality and good value, they tend to revert to familiar brands.

◪ **It provides an enduring platform on which to develop other businesses.** Brands have considerable staying power. Of the top 50 packaged goods brands in the UK, for instance, fewer than ten have been created in the past 20 years. New products can be launched under the same brand while old ones are gradually being withdrawn from the market.

Changing the elements of a successful brand can be dangerous. When British Airways changed its tail-fin design in 1997, it was part of a gentle shift in the company's branding. But the switch from variations of the Union Jack, with its nationalist overtones, to splashes of ethnic and abstract colours that were meant to convey a feeling of warmth, speed and (above all) of being part of a global community, backfired. Customers saw the new tail-fins as symbolic of a simultaneous deterioration in the airline's service. By the end of the decade, the airline had admitted the change was a mistake and had pledged to revert to variations of the UK's national flag.

When a branded product becomes number one in its market category, it is called a brand leader. There are considerable advantages to being a brand leader. An American study found that brand leaders on average achieve dramatically higher returns on investment than secondary brands.

When companies have a valuable brand they often attempt to stretch it by attaching it to other products and services. A classic example is the Mars chocolate confectionery brand, which was successfully transferred to an ice-cream product with a similar shape and flavour.

There is a theory, however, that brands can be stretched too far. The expectations that are built up in consumers by one branded product have to be delivered by all products bearing the same brand.

A brief history

Firms have recognised the power of brands for many years. One of the most fertile periods for the creation of great brands was the 1880s and 1890s, when the names of both Kodak and Kellogg first appeared in shop windows. Their inventors stumbled across a fact not fully recognised until much later: that two of the most powerful elements in a brand name are the guttural sound (and especially the "k" sound) and alliteration (repetition of the same consonant). Think of Pepsi and Coke.

Firms with international ambitions must be careful when inventing new brand names. For example, Brillo, a well-known British scouring pad, has a hard time in Italy. Brillo, in Italian, means sozzled. When Chrysler introduced its Nova car into Mexico it forgot that in Spanish *no va* means "it doesn't go".

In general, Americans have been much more successful at creating international brands than anyone else. Of the 20 most valuable brands in the world, as calculated by consultants Interbrand in 1997, no fewer than 18 were American. The exceptions were Sony (in sixth place) and Nescafé (14th). But even the most valuable brands can stumble if they do not remain sensitive to consumer tastes. When Coca-Cola, comfortably at the top of Interbrand's list, tried to launch a new formula for its main product in 1985 it flopped spectacularly, and consumers deserted the company in droves.

In recent years, the idea of branding has stretched from goods and services to individuals. Sports stars, pop stars and film stars take careful note of what brands they wear and what these brands say about them. Many modern novels describe their characters more by their clothes and accessories than by their physical features or their personalities. The brands have become shorthand for the character.

Recommended reading

Arnold, D., *The Handbook of Brand Management*, Pitman, 1992

Gilmore, F. (ed.), *Brand Warriors, Corporate Leaders Share their Winning Strategies*, HarperCollins Business, 1997

Kotler, P., *Marketing Management: Analysis, Planning and Control*, Prentice-Hall (9th edition), 1996

McRae, C., *World Class Brands*, Addison-Wesley 1990

Vishwanath, V. and Mark, J., "Your Brand's Best Strategy", *Harvard Business Review*, May–June 1997

Business cycle

Economies (and, therefore, the businesses in them) are believed to go through a regular cycle of boom and bust as they move in a generally upward direction. This idea is deep-seated and long-standing.

Discussion has generally focused not on the existence of business cycles but on their duration. Many people think that they recur every three or four years. A Russian economist, Nikolai Dimitriyevitch Kondratiev, however, thought that they roll around in phases of between 50 and 54 years.

In general, no two business cycles are alike, and some industries have their own cycles, independent of those taking place in the economy as a whole. The construction industry, for example, is notorious for the non-synchronised phasing of its waxings and wanings. Regions have their own cycles too. The East Asian economic crisis of 1997, for example, was not mirrored in the rest of the world.

Industries with high fixed costs, such as steel mills and car plants, are most vulnerable to the vicissitudes of the business cycle. They generally invest heavily when demand is strong and then find themselves with excess capacity when demand falls back. Excess capacity in an industry pushes prices down, so the profitability of a company in that industry is hit by both lower sales and lower prices. Firms can find some relief from this by using subcontractors to help out when times are good.

Economists identify four separate phases in the classic business cycle.

1 The prosperity phase, when production and sales rise, and so too do prices.
2 The liquidation phase, when consumers decide to remain liquid (that is, to save more and to consume less).
3 The recession phase, when there is widespread unemployment and business closures.
4 The recovery phase, when consumers regain their confidence.

Most explanations of the business cycle involve a switch at some stage to insufficient consumption or insufficient investment. The former can occur when prices rise so much in a boom that consumers withdraw from the market; the latter can arise when firms introduce so much extra capacity in the boom that there is too much production for the current demand. Recovery then occurs either because prices are forced down so far that consumers return to the market, or because governments stimulate the economy by themselves creating demand. This can start a virtuous circle in which consumer demand creates more jobs, which create more purchasing power, which creates more consumers.

A brief history

It is said that the Mayans of Central America were aware of the 50–54 year wave of boom and bust, and so were the ancient Israelites.

Kondratiev based his theory of long-wave cycles on a study of price changes in the 19th century. He also examined which industries suffered most during the depression phase of his cycle, and he pointed out how often technology was crucial in getting business out of that phase.

Kondratiev believed that his theory could be used to anticipate future economic developments. For his cycles have quite precise phases: the recession phase begins about 20–25 years after the boom has begun, at a time when commodity prices drop from their highs.

The current Kondratiev wave began when western economies started to pull out of the depression of the 1930s. The second world war delayed the process, but prices began to accelerate as soon as it ended. Commodity prices started dropping from their highs in the 1980s. Kondratiev theory, therefore, implies that we are about to hit the mother of all crashes.

At the end of the 20th century, however, the economies of the United States (and to a lesser extent the UK) were stuck in such a prolonged period of boom that some economists began to suggest that there was a new economic "paradigm" in operation. In it, inflation was finally defeated and old-style business cycles were overturned. Reasons given for the paradigm shift were largely related to the dramatic changes in cost structure brought about by developments in information technology, and particularly by the Internet. The Bank of England reported that these economists believed there would be significant changes in product markets as a result of the greater use of IT in distribution, of the entry of large, low-cost competitors, and of an intensification of competitive pressures.

Recommended reading

Cooley, T.F. (ed.), *Frontiers of business cycle research*, Princeton University Press, 1995

Glasner, D. (ed.), *Business cycles and Depressions: an Encyclopedia*, Garland, 1997

Kondratiev, N.D., *The Works of Nikolai D. Kondratiev*, translated by Wilson, S.S., Pickering & Chatto, 1998

Business modelling

The use of computer models to simulate different business activities and to assist in decision-making processes is almost as old as IBM itself. Business modelling was a central part of operational research (OR), a fad of the 1950s and 1960s. But it outgrew its OR roots as the mainframe came to be replaced by the PC.

Operational research (see page 161) was traditionally carried out by specialists in isolated research-style environments, but business modelling is now based on widely available software that allows non-technical general managers to try out lots of different options on (electronic) paper before deciding which one to use. A retailer, for instance, might develop a model to help it choose where to locate its new stores. It would feed in data about the size of the catchment area, local road networks, parking facilities, demographics and its local competitors. The model would then come up with the optimal locations.

Consultants KPMG say that "to take major [business] decisions without first testing their consequences in a safe environment can be likened to training an airline pilot by having him fly a 747 without first having spent months in the simulator".

Business modelling also helps to democratise decision-making by diffusing it throughout the organisation. In *Re-engineering the Corporation*, Michael Hammer wrote: "When accessible data is combined with easy-to-use analysis and modelling tools, frontline workers – when properly trained – suddenly have sophisticated decision-making capabilities. Decisions can be made more quickly and problems resolved as soon as they crop up".

Some of the biggest users of sophisticated business models are large airlines. They have to juggle with a multitude of different fare structures and to handle tricky things like stand-by tickets. Modelling such situations can save them millions of dollars a year.

Other common uses of business modelling include the following.

- ◪ Financial planning, with the help of spreadsheets. This quantifies the impact of a business decision on the balance sheet and the profit-and-loss account.
- ◪ Forecasting. Analysing historical data and using it to predict future trends (see also Scenario planning, page 190).

- Mapping processes in a visual representation of the resources required for a task and the steps to be taken to perform it.
- Data mining. Analysing vast quantities of data to dig out unpredictable relationships between variables.
- "Monte Carlo" simulation. Putting in random data to see what impact uncertainty has on the outcome of a project.

A brief history

The idea of using computer models to support decision-making was given a boost by a popular book published in 1990. Peter Senge's *The Fifth Discipline* argued that the ability to use models to experiment with corporate structure and behaviour would be a key skill in the future. He described computer simulation as "a tool for creating". Senge's "fifth discipline" is systems thinking, a notion he explained as follows:

> You can only understand the system of a rainstorm by contemplating the whole, not any individual part of the pattern ... business and other human endeavours are also systems ... systems thinking is a conceptual framework, a body of knowledge and tools, that has been developed over the past 50 years to make the full patterns clearer, and to help us see how to change them effectively.

Modelling is an integral part of this. It enables firms to go through the shift of mind that is required to get at the essence of systems thinking, namely:

- seeing the interrelationships between things rather than just straight-line chains of cause and effect; and
- seeing the processes of change, not just snapshots of one particular moment in time.

Senge also promoted the idea of using modelling to create what he called "Microworlds". These are simplified simulation models packaged as management games. They allow managers to "play" with an issue in safety rather than playing with it in the real world. The rapidly expanding power of the PC, the development of new modelling techniques and the growth of things like virtual reality will probably take business modelling into completely new areas in the 21st century. Here managers will be able to play increasingly sophisticated market games, with virtual customers and virtual products, before they have to go out into the real world and do the real thing.

Recommended reading

Checkland, P., *Systems Thinking; Systems Practice*, John Wiley, 1981
Senge, P.M., *The Fifth Discipline*, Doubleday, 1990

The business plan

In one sense this is the written fantasy about the future of a new business that has to be documented if it is ever to get the financial support that 99.9% of such businesses require. A business plan is not just a matter of qualitative fantasising, however, of asserting that "We intend to be innovative market leaders at the leading edge of Internet technology", for example. It is also a matter of quantitative fantasising, "and we will make a loss of $1.64m in year one, and a profit of $325,000 in year two". The launching of a business idea requires its patron to attribute precise financial numbers to the future cash flow of the business – numbers, needless to say, that rarely bear any relationship to subsequent reality.

So what is the point? It is generally accepted that there are two.

1 To obtain funds. Every investor and/or venture capitalist wants to read a business plan to help them assess the likely risk and reward of the project. For the infant business seeking finance, the presentation of a business plan is a bit like an actor's audition. There are notoriously bad ones, and a good one is no guarantee of a part. But with a bad one, you are almost sure never to see the footlights.

2 To help the business's promoters focus on some fundamental operational issues. For example, what is the likely size of their market? Who is likely to be their main competitor? To some extent the setting of operational targets for the venture's team is self-fulfilling. If the venture is successful, then the targets set are the targets reached. They may not be the optimal performance of the organisation, of course, merely a satisfactory one.

Business plans are required not only by new business ventures but also by old businesses trying something new. For example, proposed mergers and acquisitions require a detailed plan of the future of the merged entity; a venture into a new market requires a business plan; and so too does the winding down or the turning round of an old and tired business.

In an influential article in the *Harvard Business Review*, a professor of business administration, William Sahlman, suggested that business plans "waste too much ink on numbers and devote too little to the information that really matters to intelligent investors". What really matters, suggested Sahlman, are four factors that are "critical to every new venture":

- the people;
- the opportunity;
- the context; and
- risk and reward.

A great business plan, Sahlman suggests, is one that focuses on asking the right questions about these four things. It is not easy to compose, however, because "most entrepreneurs are wild-eyed optimists". Anyway, as he says, "The market is as fickle as it is unpredictable. Who would have guessed that plug-in room deodorisers would sell?"

A brief history

Throughout much of the 20th century a business plan was widely accepted as being indispensable for new business ventures. Once upon a time Microsoft had one, and so did Cisco Systems and Dell Computer. But towards the end of the century the traditional form of the business plan was questioned in the light of the rapid changes in markets brought about by information technology, telecommunications and the Internet. Many companies found the techniques of scenario planning (see page 190) more helpful in such an environment; others turned to computer-based business modelling (see page 18) to help them take account of their environment's fast-changing multitude of variables.

Recommended reading

Cooper, G., *The Business Plan Workbook*, Prentice-Hall, 1989

Cross, W. and Richey, A.M., *The Prentice-Hall Encyclopaedia of Model Business Plans*, Prentice-Hall, 1998

Kahrs, K. and Kahrs, P. (eds), *Business Plans Handbook, a Compilation of Actual Business Plans Developed by Small Businesses throughout North America*, Gale, 1995

O'Hara, P., *The Total Business Plan*, John Wiley, 1990

Sahlman, W.A., "How to Write a Great Business Plan", *Harvard Business Review*, July-August 1997

The C curve

Economics has its J curve: the "it's got to get worse before it gets better" relationship between exchange rates and the balance of payments. The immediate effect of a currency's depreciation is a deterioration in the balance of payments (the dip in the J), which occurs before it starts to improve (when it moves on to the longer limb of the letter).

Management too has an "it's got to get worse before it gets better" curve. It is called the C curve, and it plots the relationship between corporate growth and reconstruction. In general, it says that companies with low profitability reach an impasse, a point where they have to shrink and restructure before they can hope to grow again. The decision on which course this reconstruction should take and, more importantly, to what extent and for how long, is one of the major causes of internal strategic tension within corporations.

The idea was developed in the 1990s by the Boston Consulting Group (BCG). In a study of successful and unsuccessful corporate turnarounds (changes from low profitability to high profitability), BCG found that there were a number of features common to the successful cases.

- They raised their profitability well above the hurdle rate (the rate needed to give a better return to investors than could be gained from putting money into government securities).
- They often had to go through quite dramatic restructurings – a reduction in their investment base of as much as 25% and a doubling or tripling of their return on capital employed.
- They often spent as long as two or three years on restructuring before they turned their minds back to growth again.

The C curve appears when the company's capital employed is plotted against the return on that capital. It starts off at a low level (this is the definition of a company with low profitability). At first the capital employed shrinks without there being any improvement in the return. So the curve goes more or less horizontally backwards, like the beginnings of a C. Then, if the restructuring is being successful, the returns start to improve. (If the restructuring is not successful the company is in serious trouble.) At this point the graph moves sharply upwards, along the left-hand stroke of the C. After this has gone on for an appropriate period, the company can start to invest again and go for growth. Then the capital employed increases and the graph moves sharply to the right, the final stroke of the C.

BCG found that companies which did not make a successful turnaround often rushed into growth too early. Their Cs were short and flat, and they dipped down again sharply at the end. Hence they returned almost to the point where they began – that is, they were a bit like an O and a waste of time. For a successful turnaround, companies needed to chart the course of a tall and well-rounded C.

A brief history

The theory was developed against the background of the recession and corporate downsizing of the early 1990s, followed by the remarkable rebound in American stockmarkets in the second half of the decade. Europe followed somewhat behind in this process. Its recession was later, and its rebound had still not fully appeared by the end of the century.

The extent of this difference was highlighted in a BCG study of the value created by European and American quoted companies in the five years from 1994 to 1998. In terms of the average annual growth in shareholder returns over the period, American companies were streets ahead. Six out of the top ten and 16 out of the top 20 performers were American.

The performance of the United States was different not only quantitatively but also qualitatively. Over the period, American companies created far more shareholder value by means of growth than did European companies. The Europeans relied more on restructuring to create value

Several conclusions were drawn from the study, one of them being that growth was a far more powerful creator of value than was restructuring. The gains to be made from brand new investment were far greater than those to be made from squeezing extra juice out of old investment. At least they were during the period of the study.

Another conclusion was that Europe's turn had yet to come. The European companies that were busily restructuring in the late 1990s should be able to blossom into a brand new phase of growth in the early years of the 21st century.

Cannibalisation

When a firm introduces a new product or service into a market where there is little scope for further growth, that product or service will either eat into the share of the market's existing products or swiftly disappear from sight. If some of the existing products are manufactured by the firm that is introducing the new product, then the newcomers will cannibalise the old timers; that is, they will eat into the market share of their own kind. For example, it has been estimated that two-thirds of the sales of Gillette's Sensor razor came from consumers who would otherwise have been customers for the company's other razors.

There are sound reasons for firms to want to do such a seemingly stupid thing. In the first place, they may need to keep ahead of the competition. In the chocolate bar market in the UK, for instance, the decline in Kit Kat's share was arrested by the launch of a new, more chunky bar, which undoubtedly cannibalised the market for the original. Its appeal was to all those people who buy chocolate bars, including those who bought the old Kit Kat.

Firms may also choose to cannibalise their own products by producing marginally improved products. The idea is to persuade existing customers to purchase an upgraded version. This is true of the PC market, for example, where Intel's newest, most powerful processor cannibalises the last generation of Intel processors, but in the interests of arresting any decline in the total market.

Economists sometimes distinguish between planned and unplanned cannibalisation. Planned cannibalisation is an anticipated loss in sales of an existing product as a result of the introduction of a new product in the same line. In the unplanned version, the loss of sales from an established product to a more recently introduced one is unexpected.

A brief history

Historically, firms have found it hard to cannibalise their own products. They often try to hang on to declining market shares for too long before deciding to introduce new products that compete with their own. Kodak, for example, refused for years to introduce the 35mm camera for fear of cannibalising its older products.

The Internet presented many firms with difficult decisions about cannibalisation. Travel agents, for instance, had to decide whether to offer online services at a fraction of the cost of their traditional branch-based services in order to compete with airlines and other firms that were beginning to sell to customers via direct online links.

Deregulation also presented companies with difficult dilemmas about cannibalising products and services that had thrived for years in protected markets. In the airline business, for example, traditional national carriers were faced with feisty, low-cost new entrants. In response, British Airways for one introduced its own low-cost airline. It competed not only with the new entrants but also (in a carefully controlled way) with BA itself.

Recommended reading

Kerin, R. and Peterson, R., *Strategic Marketing Problems: Cases & Comments*, Prentice-Hall (8th edition), 1998

Championing

To champion something is to support it, to defend it. We champion the cause of liberty. Ladybird Johnson, wife of the American president who succeeded John F. Kennedy, championed the cause of wild flowers.

The word was given a management twist in the late 20th century when many companies came to believe that each new project, in order to gain success, needed a champion, a specific individual within the organisation who would defend it and nurture it through its early days. Without such a person, it was suggested, a new project would wither from lack of devotion.

Edward Schon of the Massachusetts Institute of Technology (MIT) wrote:

> The new idea either finds a champion or dies ... No
> ordinary involvement with a new idea provides the energy
> required to cope with the indifference and resistance that
> major technological change provokes ... Champions of new
> inventions display persistence and courage of heroic quality.

Championing is often applied to people as well: bright, young, talented people within an organisation are deemed to need a champion, someone higher up the corporate ladder who will support them and fight their corner. Many chief executives have risen to the top largely because they have been nurtured throughout their careers by people in high places.

In their book *In Search of Excellence*, Tom Peters and Robert Waterman say that successfully innovative companies revolve around "fired-up champions". The American inventor of the Post-It note, 3M, told them: "We expect our champions to be irrational."

Champions are not easy people to work and live with. James Brian Quinn spells out a paradox associated with the type:

> The champion is obnoxious, impatient, egotistic, and
> perhaps a bit irrational in organisational terms. As a
> consequence, he is not hired. If hired, he is not promoted or
> rewarded. He is regarded as not a serious person, as
> embarrassing or disruptive.

Peters and Waterman maintain that companies need to set up special systems to support and encourage these disruptive people if they are to benefit from their stubborn persistence with new ideas (not necessarily their own).

A brief history

Championing is held to be particularly important in the process of innovation (see page 116), of bringing an invention to market. History is spattered with innovations that would never have been successful in a marketplace if they had not been stubbornly supported by one (often rather cranky) individual.

A widely reported case was that of Spence Silver, an employee of 3M, who became unusually fond of a glue that was not very good at gluing. "I was just absolutely convinced that it had some potential," Silver is reported as saying. But for many years he was unable to persuade anybody else within the organisation to agree with him. He persisted, however, in championing his pet product. As he himself put it:

> You have to be a zealot at times in order to keep interest alive, because it will die off. It seems like the pattern always goes like this. In the fat times, these groups appear and do a lot of interesting research. And then the lean times come just about at the point when you've developed your first goody, your gizmo. And then you've got to go out and try to sell it. Well, everybody in the division is so busy that they don't want to touch it. They don't have time to look at new product ideas with no end-product already in mind.

Spence Silver's persistence with his "glue that doesn't glue" eventually led to the invention of the Post-It note. The rest, as they say, is history.

Recommended reading

Peters, T. and Waterman, R., *In Search of Excellence*, Harper & Row, 1982
Nayak, P. Ranganath and Ketteringham, J.M., *Breakthroughs*, Rawson Associates, 1986

Change management

Businesses are perpetually torn between their desire to define for all time their organisation's structure and strategy, and their recognition that their world is in a constant state of flux. For the larger part of the 20th century they were more concerned with the static elements of this dichotomy. Only in later years did they come to focus on the dynamic side, on how to manage and live with the change that was inevitably making redundant their latest business plans, even as the ink dried on them.

This change can take many forms: a decline in market share, for instance, because of cost-cutting by new rivals; or a new technology (such as the mobile phone) that transforms a market or two. Learning to live with all this is the art of change management.

Traditionally, a business project had a specified beginning, middle and end. The once influential idea of management by objectives (see page 141), for example, demands that managers know precisely where they are going before they set out on a journey. Once change is taken into account, however, that journey has to be broken up into a series of small steps. Each of these has a beginning, a middle and an end, and leads not to some grand immutable goal, but only to whatever is the next appropriate step. In this world, managers have to learn to live with uncertainty, to set out without knowing where they might end up.

Previously, of course, they believed that they knew where they were going only to find that, more often than not, projects had to be changed even as they progressed. This led to boundless management frustration with a perceived failure to reach agreed goals.

In a classic analysis of the dilemma, a business professor, Henry Mintzberg, described how a student asked him whether he "was intending to play jigsaw puzzle or Lego" with all the elements of structure and power that he had described in his books and that he had put together to make a number of configurations of different organisations. Mintzberg wrote:

> In other words, did I mean all these elements of
> organisations to fit together in set ways – to create known
> images [the static state] – or were they to be used creatively
> to build new ones [the dynamic state]? I had to answer that
> I had been promoting jigsaw puzzles, even if I was suggesting
> that the pieces could be combined into several images

> *instead of the usual one. But I immediately began to think about playing organisational Lego. Configuration is a nice thing when you can have it. Unfortunately, some organisations all of the time, and all organisations some of the time, cannot.*

Lego stands you in better stead in an ever-changing world.

A brief history

Rosabeth Moss Kanter is a Harvard academic who is probably best known for her work on change management. Her book, *The Change Masters*, was labelled as "the thinking man's *In Search of Excellence*", the more popular title by Tom Peters and Robert Waterman that came out a year earlier. Charles Handy, another business writer who has focused closely on change management, has identified "discontinuous change" as the only constant characteristic in today's workplace.

The focus on change led to a host of analogies between business organisations and the biological world. In the biological world, adapting to change (in climate and environment) is the oldest game in town.

This close examination of the nature of change and the search for a suitable analogy had its critics. In *Beyond the Hype, Rediscovering the Essence of Management*, Robert Eccles and Nitui Nohria said that "the primary concern of managers ... should be mobilising action among individuals, rather than endless quibbling about the way the world really is". The nature of change, they felt, was being discussed more than the question of how to manage businesses and the people in them.

Recommended reading

Carr, D.K., Hurd, K.J. and Trahant, W.J., *Managing the Change Process*, McGraw Hill, 1996

Drucker, P., *Managing in a Time of Great Change*, Butterworth Heinemann, 1995

Eisenhardt, K. and Brown, S., "Time Pacing: Competing in Markets That Won't Stand Still", *Harvard Business Review*, March-April 1998

Eisenhardt, K. and Brown, S., *Competing on the Edge: Strategy as Structured Chaos*, Harvard Business School Press, 1998

Kanter, R.M., *The Change Masters*, Simon & Schuster, 1983

Mintzberg, H., *Mintzberg on Management*, Free Press, 1989

Sadler, P., *Managing Change*, Kogan Page, 1995

The Journal of Organisational Change Management

Cherry-picking

The idea of cherry-picking has been applied in a number of business contexts. It is, for example, applied to customers who ignore products that are bundled together by a manufacturer (who in the process may disguise cross-subsidies between high-margin and low-margin components of the bundle). Such customers prefer to bundle their products together for themselves, selecting the best (that is, cherry-picking) from each category of component.

An obvious example is the purchase of music systems. Manufacturers sell music sets, made up of an amplifier, a tape deck, a CD player, speakers and a tuner. But many music enthusiasts choose to assemble their own sets, buying their amplifier, tape deck, speakers and so on each from a different producer. Manufacturers try to discourage consumers from behaving in this way by making the price of the complete set competitive. But earnest cherry-pickers can usually find discounted components that enable them to assemble something cheaper.

The term cherry-picking is also applied to the behaviour of new entrants into old industries, firms which try to choose their customers carefully. By calculating which consumers are profitable (and appealing to them and ignoring those who are not) such a firm can sometimes rapidly gain market share. In some cases, cherry-pickers are successful because traditional firms in the industry do not know who their profitable customers are.

Service industries are particularly vulnerable. It is difficult for them to measure the profitability of individual customers and customer segments. So they are never quite sure what they want to keep and what they want to get rid of. Successful cherry-pickers leave an industry's incumbents with the least profitable customers. They also push up the price to consumers who are not attractive to the cherry-pickers. In car insurance, for example, cherry-picking in the UK pushed up the price prohibitively for young drivers in the 1990s.

A brief history

A number of new airlines set about cherry-picking when deregulation of the skies in Europe and the United States allowed them into the market. Within limits, they were able choose which routes to operate on. They were unencumbered with the obligations that the traditional national flag-carrier airlines had to bear in the interests of government policies on transport and/or regional development. Virgin, which cherry-picked the London-New York run, was one such airline.

In banking and insurance, cherry-picking newcomers were able to undermine the business of old-timers in just a few years at the end of the 20th century. Firms such as Direct Line, a British telesales insurance business, rapidly won market share by focusing on a narrow (profitable) segment of the market and avoiding costly traditional distribution channels.

The success of cherry-pickers emphasises something known as the survivorship bias: the tendency to judge the past by the record of relatively long-term survivors, ignoring those who drowned or those who made their entrance in the meanwhile. In 1999 the survivors in an industry (those whose performance could be compared over, say, a ten-year time frame) were less representative of that industry than at any other time in the 20th century.

Recommended reading

Goetzmann, W. and Jorian, P., "History as written by the winners", *Forbes*, June 16th 1997

Clustering

Clustering is an idea that has been transferred from economics to management and business. It is the phenomenon (and the explanation for it) whereby firms from the same industry gather together in close proximity. Clustering is particularly evident in industries like banking. Banking centres in cities such as London and New York have thrived for centuries. Some hundreds of banks have clustered there, close together and within easy walking distance of each other.

Economists explain clustering as a means for small companies to enjoy some of the economies of scale (see page 76) usually reserved for big companies. By sticking together they are able to benefit from such things as the neighbourhood's pool of expertise and skilled workers; its easy access to component suppliers; and its information channels (both formal ones like trade magazines and informal ones like everyday gossip).

Modern high-tech clusters often gather around prestigious universities on whose research they can piggyback. Silicon Valley is near Stanford University, and there are similar high-tech clusters around Harvard University near Boston in the United States and around Cambridge University in the UK.

A greenfield site in a depressed region where government grants are plentiful may bring a young company immediate benefits. But in the longer term, strange though it may sound, the young company may be better off squeezing itself on to an expensive piece of real estate in close proximity to a significant number of its competitors.

A brief history

One of the most famous clusters of all is the film industry in Hollywood. When the big studio system broke up in the 1930s it fractured into a large number of what were essentially small specialist firms and freelancers. The Hollywood cluster allows each of these small units to benefit as if it had the scale of an old movie studio, but without the rigidities of the studios' wage hierarchy and unionised labour.

In some cases, the ancillary services that grew up to service industrial clusters have remained in position and developed into vibrant new industries long after their original client industry has faded. Near Birmingham, in the UK, for instance, the cluster of car-industry service firms that grew up when that city was a force in the car industry has become a key element in the development of Formula One and other specialist vehicle businesses.

Evidence that clustering is not a phenomenon whose time has been and gone is provided by examples such as California's Silicon Valley. New IT and Internet firms continue to gather there in spite of the high prices of local property and the dangers of earthquakes. Furthermore, much of the most valuable information that they obtain comes not electronically but from face-to-face meetings.

Michael Porter, a professor at Harvard Business School whose insights into the nature of competition between firms were highly influential in the 1980s and 1990s (see Competitive advantage, page 35), has turned his attention to this seemingly paradoxical revival of industrial clusters. He said recently that, in theory, location should no longer be a source of competitive advantage in an era of global competition, rapid transport and high-speed communications. The world's increasingly global businesses should by now be above and beyond geography. Yet there are as many instances of a critical mass of firms with a common thread clustering together as there ever were.

Porter gives several (non-silicon) examples, including the wine-growing industry in northern California and the flower-growing business in the Netherlands. The Netherlands would not be the natural first choice for anyone starting a flower-growing business today were it not for the fact that the business is already there. This is a huge competitive advantage for a new entrant, who can benefit from such things as the sophisticated Dutch flower auctions, the flower-growers' associations and the advanced research centres.

Recommended reading

Porter, M., "Clusters and the New Economics of Competition", *Harvard Business Review*, November-December 1998

Competitive advantage

Competitive Advantage is the title of a book by Michael Porter, a Harvard Business School professor, which in the late 1980s became the bible of business thinkers. With its echoes of the popular ideas of comparative advantage expounded by a 19th-century economist, David Ricardo, it provided managers with a framework for strategic thinking about how to beat their competitors. Porter argued that:

> *Competitive advantage is a function of either providing comparable buyer value more efficiently than competitors (low cost), or performing activities at comparable cost but in unique ways that create more buyer value than competitors and, hence, command a premium price (differentiation).*

You win by being cheaper, or you win by being different (which means being perceived by the customer as better or more relevant). There are no other ways.

Few management ideas have been so clear or so intuitively right. Although there have been business and management books that sold more copies in the last two decades of the 20th century, none has been as influential as *Competitive Advantage*.

Behind competitive advantage lay a novel way of looking at the firm as a series of activities which link together into what Porter called "a value chain" (see page 231). For many readers, this was the eureka moment in the theory. Many writers have since developed concepts based on the metaphor of a linked chain of activities or groups of activities (or their close equivalent, processes, see page 179). Each of the links in the chain adds value, that is, something that customers are prepared to pay for. Even a company's support activities, such as training and compensation systems, can be links in the chain and sources of competitive advantage in their own right.

A brief history

Competition, and the ways in which one firm wins and another loses, has been a subject of study for decades. But there had been little focus on the competitive behaviour of the individual firm before Porter's work.

Competitive Advantage was published in 1985 as "the essential companion" to Porter's earlier work, *Competitive Strategy* (1980). *Competitive Strategy* considered competition at the industry level, but *Competitive Advantage* looked at it from a firm's-eye view. "My quest", said Porter, "was to find a way to conceptualise the firm that would expose the underpinnings of competitive advantage and its sustainability."

Competitive Strategy (subtitled "Techniques for Analysing Industries and Competitors") was an aide for ambitious young executives in the planning department to help them come up with grand ideas about what to do next. The book defined five factors that have an impact on a company's profitability: customers, suppliers, substitutes, potential entrants into the industry, and competitors.

Competitive Advantage, however, was for the chief executive. Its subtitle was "Creating and Sustaining Superior Performance". Not only did it promise to enable senior managers to get ahead of the competition, it was also going to help them to stay there. "Sustainability" became a buzz word. The remedy sounded like no less than corporate Viagra.

Porter's activity-based view of the firm has been used to give concrete meaning to the historically woolly idea of synergy (see page 218). As he put it:

> *The ability to add value through competing in multiple*
> *businesses can be understood in terms of sharing activities*
> *or transferring proprietary skills across activities. This allows*
> *the elusive notion of synergy to be made concrete and*
> *rigorous.*

The ideas in *Competitive Advantage* persuaded corporate chiefs to undertake more internal reflection. Previously, their firm's identity was often described in terms of its relationship to others: its market share, for instance, or its relative size. Porter made corporate navel-gazing respectable. In practice, many firms had difficulty in identifying all the discrete Porterian activities in their organisation, even in cases where they were confident that they knew what they were looking for – and many were not.

In a later book, *The Competitive Advantage of Nations*, Porter looked at how the choice of location by an internationalising business might be a source of competitive advantage. From this issue of location he was drawn on to consider clustering (see page 33) and how business clusters are nowadays "critical to competition". In 1998 he listed the subjects of his current research as being: "Why do activity differences leading to distinct competitive positions arise? When do trade-offs occur between positions? What makes activities hard to imitate? How do activities fit together? How are unique positions developed over time?"

Apart from being a best-selling author, Porter founded a management consulting firm, Monitor, through which all his consulting activities are channelled. He can command as much as $100,000 for a one-hour presentation. His personal competitive weapon is differentiation, not low cost.

Recommended reading

Porter, M., "How Competitive Forces Shape Strategy", *Harvard Business Review*, March-April 1979

Porter, M., *Competitive Strategy, Techniques for Analysing Industries and Competitors*, Free Press, 1980

Porter, M., *Competitive Advantage, Creating and Sustaining Superior Performance*, Free Press, 1985

Porter, M., *The Competitive Advantage of Nations*, Free Press, 1990

Stalk, G., "Time: The Next Source of Competitive Advantage", *Harvard Business Review*, July-August 1988

Convergence

Convergence refers to the way in which the requirements to enter different industries become so similar that firms can just as easily take part in one as in the other. One of the areas where convergence was evident in the 1990s was banking and insurance. So common was the phenomenon of banks getting into the insurance business that the practice was given a name: "bankassurance". In utilities, too, convergence became increasingly common with the deregulation and privatisation of many industries in the sector. In general, convergence had the effect of greatly increasing competition.

There were two main reasons for this outbreak of convergence.

◪ Companies were finding that their own markets were too crowded. IT and deregulation enabled impudent new entrants to do things that would have been unthinkable a decade before. Firms felt they needed to move into new fields to find some breathing space.

  This was particularly obvious in banking. In a number of European countries the degree of concentration in the industry was such that firms had few domestic takeover options that would not have incurred the wrath of the anti-trust authorities. In effect, they were forced to vegetate or to go elsewhere.

◪ As firms became more customer-focused, they realised that customers who trusted them to supply one type of product or service were inclined to trust them to supply many more. In utilities, for example, big customers in the United States increasingly turned to companies like Enron that could supply them with all their energy needs. Given the choice, many of them preferred the convenience of a single supplier.

The convergence of industries produced firms that looked much like the conglomerates formed by the periodic enthusiasms for diversification (see page 66). But the motivation for the creation of these conglomerates was very different from that which formed conglomerates in the 1960s. Diversification then was driven by a desire to spread financial risk, largely for the benefit of shareholders. The conglomerates formed through convergence were driven by a desire to please consumers in a world where the balance of power between buyer and supplier was changing rapidly. Customers wanted convenience above all things, and one way of getting it was by buying as wide a range of goods and services as possible from a trusted single supplier.

A brief history

As the utility industries (electricity, gas, telephone, water) were deregulated in the 1980s and 1990s, firms found that they required a hard core of competencies to run any one of them. These included sophisticated metering and billing services, a tightly controlled fleet of maintenance vans, and call centres that could deal with orders and customer queries. This made firms that sold gas to retail customers feel competent to offer them electricity (bought wholesale from a deregulated manufacturer). Power generators went into electricity distribution, and water companies seemed to flow everywhere.

The greatest convergence among utilities occurred in the gas and electricity sectors. In 1998 Andersen Consulting reckoned that, within ten years, 40% of Europe's electricity would be produced from gas. At the time, under 15% of it was. In the United States the figure was almost 75%, with Andersen reckoning that 14 of the 30 largest gas and electricity firms in the United States had made convergence-related acquisitions or mergers in the two years from 1996 to 1998.

Convergence also occurred in other industries. An Italian computer company, Olivetti, for example, paid $65 billion in 1999 for Telecom Italia, a telecommunications company six times its size. Olivetti, originally one of the world's best-known typewriter brands, had already reinvented itself once as a personal-computer company before it chose to move in such a big way into telecommunications.

Recommended reading

Dollar, D. and Wolff, E.N., *Competitiveness, Convergence and International Specialisation*, MIT Press, 1993

Whitley, R. and Kristensen, P.H. (eds), *The Changing European Firm: Limits to Convergence*, Routledge, 1996

Core competence

A core competence is a set of skills that have been integrated in a unique way by a firm in order to add value. The idea of core competence was first introduced into management literature in 1990 by C.K. Prahalad and Gary Hamel. The two business academics wrote:

> Core competencies are the collective learning in the organisation, especially how to co-ordinate diverse production skills and integrate multiple streams of technologies ... core competence is communication, involvement and a deep commitment to working across organisational boundaries ... core competence does not diminish with use. Unlike physical assets, which do deteriorate over time, competencies are enhanced as they are applied and shared.

Prahalad and Hamel went on to outline three tests to be applied to determine whether something is a core competence.

- First, a core competence provides potential access to a wide variety of markets.
- Second, a core competence should make a significant contribution to the perceived customer benefits of the end product.
- Third, a core competence should be difficult for competitors to imitate. And it will be difficult if it is a complex harmonisation of individual technologies and production skills.

The two academics painted a picture of the corporation as a tree whose roots are its particular competencies. Out of these roots grow the organisation's "core products" which, in turn, nourish a number of separate business units. Lastly, out of these business units come "end products".

It was Prahalad and Hamel's contention that if a company could "maintain world manufacturing dominance in core products", then it would "reserve the power to shape the evolution of end products". Many of the examples on which they based their theories were large, successful Japanese companies. Before the end of the century, however, the performance of these companies had become distinctly less stellar.

The core competence idea was useful not only for focusing on essentials, but also for identifying those things that were not "at the core". Why, management might ask, were these non-essential things being allowed to consume valuable resources?

The ideas surrounding core competence were, arguably, the first significant steps in strategic thinking since Michael Porter powerfully diverted chief executives' attention away from market share and on to value chains (see page 231) and business activities. Prahalad and Hamel succeeded in persuading them to look at strategy as something more fluid and less precise. Their writing is spattered with references to things like "strategic intent", "strategy as stretch and leverage", "competitive space" and "expeditionary markets". Porter had turned strategic thinking back towards scientific management (see page 193) and Frederick Taylor; Prahalad and Hamel changed that direction by several degrees.

A brief history

The drive to identify a firm's core competencies, the things that it does uniquely well, became particularly strong in the 1990s alongside the growing popularity of outsourcing (see page 163). When companies were suddenly able to outsource almost any process that came under their corporate umbrella, they needed to know what was the sacred core of activities that only they could carry out, the activities that it made no sense for them to hand over to a third party. In some cases the answer was very few, and such companies were then free to become virtual organisations (see page 235).

The idea spread from core competence to core everything – core processes, core skills – everything that constituted the essence of what a company was and did. Management advisers stressed that companies needed to focus on their core as part of a process of self-awareness. Only by being self-aware, understanding their strengths and their weaknesses, could companies hope to understand how they might add value in a business environment of fast change and unpredictability.

Recommended reading

Drucker, P., *Managing in a Time of Great Change*, Butterworth-Heinemann, 1995

Goddard, J., "The Architecture of Core Competence" *Business Strategy Review*, Vol. 1, 1997

Lei, D. and Hitt, M.A., "Dynamic Core Competence Through Rota

Learning and Strategic Context", *Journal of Management*, Vol. 22, No. 4, 1996

Prahalad, C.K. and Hamel, G., "The Core Competence of the Corporation", *Harvard Business Review*, May-June 1990

Prahalad, C.K. and Hamel, G., *Competing for the Future*, HBR Press, 1994

www.hq.nasa.gov/office/hqlibrary/ppm/ppm25.htm

Cost-benefit analysis

Cost-benefit analysis is the weighing-scale approach to reaching business decisions: all the pluses (the benefits) are put on one side of the balance and all the minuses (the costs) are put on the other. Whichever weighs the heavier wins. If the costs weigh more, the proposal gets the thumbs down; if the benefits weigh more, it gets the thumbs up. For example, a company considering whether to buy new computer systems might attempt a cost-benefit analysis to help it make up its mind. On the cost side there would be things like:

- the price of the computers themselves;
- the cost of hiring people to install them;
- the cost of training staff to use them.

On the benefits side there would be things like:

- greater speed in carrying out the company's operations;
- greater efficiency in organising data;
- a boost to staff morale from using the latest equipment.

All of us do intuitive cost-benefit analyses every day of our lives. For example, "Shall I take a taxi to my next meeting or will I not save enough time for it to be worth my while?" The technique is also used extensively by industry and commerce. Nevertheless, this comparatively simple idea has complicated ramifications. The pluses and minuses are not all immediately obvious, and many of them are not easily measurable in monetary terms. How, for instance, do you put a monetary value on an increase in staff morale?

Moreover, decisions cannot be made in isolation. There are usually several competing options: if you do not invest in a new plant in west Africa you can increase capacity at your existing plant, or you can take over a new business, or you can just leave the money in the bank. It is the proposal with the highest net benefit that gets the go-ahead.

A brief history
Benjamin Franklin, inventor of the lightning conductor and co-author of the American Declaration of Independence, was a practitioner of cost-

benefit analysis. In 1772, he wrote:

> *When difficult cases occur, they are difficult chiefly because while we have them under consideration, all the reasons pro and con are not present to the mind at the same time ... To get over this, my way is to divide half a sheet of paper by a line into two columns; writing over the one "Pro", and the other "Con". Then ... I put down under the different heads short hints of the different motives ... for and against the measure ... I endeavour to estimate their respective weights; where I find one on each side that seem equal, I strike them both out. If I find a reason pro equal to two reasons con, I strike out three ... and thus proceeding I find at length where the balance lies ... And, though the weight of reasons cannot be taken with the precision of algebraic quantities, yet when each is thus considered, separately and comparatively, and the whole lies before me, I think I can judge better, and am less liable to take a rash step.*

In recent years, cost-benefit analysis has been widely used for analysing public-sector projects, as a tool to help answer questions such as: "Should we subsidise the sale of things like unleaded petrol and solar panels?" or "Shall we turn this busy urban street into a pedestrian zone?" In these examples, the social costs are the most important ones. What are the benefits to human health of reducing the levels of lead in the atmosphere? And can you measure this – for example, in terms of the medical facilities that will not be required as a result of the better health of the population?

Recommended reading

Layard, R. and Glaister, S., *Cost-Benefit Analysis*, Cambridge University Press (2nd edition), 1994

Mishan, E.J., *Cost-Benefit Analysis, an Informal Introduction*, Allen & Unwin, 1982

Roy, A., *Cost-Benefit Analysis: Theory and Application*, Johns Hopkins University Press, 1984

Crisis management

The Institute for Crisis Management (ICM), an American consulting firm that specialises in developing communications strategies for crisis-struck businesses, defines a crisis as "a significant business disruption which stimulates extensive news media coverage. The resulting public scrutiny will affect the organisation's normal operations and also could have a political, legal, financial and governmental impact on its business".

The idea that businesses face moments of crisis that require special skills not called upon in the more normal course of commercial events is widely accepted. Allied to it is the idea that there are people who are especially good at handling crises, and that there are crisis management skills that can be learned. Special training courses on the subject can be found in many countries.

Crises are commonplace. The ICM has a database of some 60,000 stories of business crises, and its records go back only to 1990. From an analysis of this database, the institute puts the causes of crises into four categories:

- Acts of God (storms, earthquakes, etc).
- Mechanical problems (metal fatigue, etc).
- Human errors (the wrong valve opened, miscommunication, etc).
- Management decisions/indecision (underestimating a problem, assuming nobody will find out).

The ICM reckons that over 60% of crises fall into the last category.

There are several important elements in good crisis management.

Be well prepared in advance
Companies should be ready to form a crisis management team at short notice. Potential members of the team should rehearse how they would manage the impact of an incident on the company and on its employees. It is a bit like learning the safety instructions on a plane before take-off: you hope you will never need them, but you know you would be a fool to miss the lesson.

The members of the team should be determined by the nature of the incident, but it should (at least) include the chief executive or a senior manager and a representative of the press office (or someone skilled at handling press enquiries). All external enquiries relating to the crisis should be answered by the team. In the case of the crash of a British Midland jet in the UK, for example, the company's chairman, Sir Michael Bishop, became the spokesman for the incident.

Move fast
It is the first few hours that count, the period when news of the crisis first breaks. Everyone will build on the information that is disclosed during that time. One of the most difficult things is handling the ambiguity in those first hours and days after a crisis breaks. There will be gaps and inconsistencies in the information available.

Get outside help and advice
Because a crisis is often brought on by employees of the firm, it can be difficult for insiders to view the issue objectively. Outside help can provide this objectivity.

Be honest
Accurate and correct information is vital. Misinformation invariably backfires on the company. But if the company has a naturally secretive culture this is a difficult policy for it to pursue, even at the best of times. Information has to be transmitted not only to the outside media but also to the firm's own staff, for they will inevitably talk to outsiders and the media themselves.

Look to the long term
Do not seek to contain only the short-term losses. A contaminated product may require the withdrawal of massive stocks in the short term to reassure customers over the longer term that the product is safe for consumption. In the case of contaminated Coca-Cola cans in Belgium and France in June 1999, the Belgian government was not convinced that the drinks company had been sufficiently swift in its response. As a result, it imposed more severe restrictions than it might otherwise have done.

A brief history

In recent years, certain industries have been more prone to crises than others. Tobacco companies have been in an almost permanent state of crisis as the medical evidence against them has unfolded over the years. Oil companies have a crisis on their hands every time one of their tankers leaves a slick on a beautiful stretch of coastline.

One of the worst environmental accidents so far, at the Union Carbide factory in India where thousands of people were killed by a leak of poisonous gas in 1984, made companies everywhere think again about how to manage crises on such a scale. Then the Exxon Valdez oil spill of 1989, generally regarded as one of the worst-managed crises of all time, showed how it should not be done.

It took two weeks for Exxon's chief executive, Lawrence Rawl, to visit the scene and make any kind of substantive statement regarding the tragedy. As the *Financial Times* put it: "This sent a clear message about where mass pollution figured on Rawl's priorities, despite his insistence that he was staying away in order not to hinder the clean-up operation." As well as the damage to its reputation as a leading oil company, the crisis cost Exxon approximately $1 billion for the clean-up, plus an additional $3 billion in compensatory and punitive damages forced upon it by the courts in Alaska. The punitive damages would have been considerably less if the company had shown more concern in the immediate aftermath of the accident.

Recommended reading

Irvine, R., *When You Are The Headline*, Institute for Crisis Management, 1991

Meyers, G.C. and Holusha, J., *When It Hits the Fan*, Houghton Mifflin, 1986

Mitroff, I.I. *et al*, *The Essential Guide to Managing Corporate Crises*, Oxford University Press, 1996

Regester, M. and Larkin, J., *Risk issues and crisis management*, Kogan Page, 1997

Sikich, G.W., *Emergency Planning Handbook*, McGraw-Hill, 1995

Institute for Crisis Management
Watertower Square
400 Missouri Avenue, Suite 101
Clarksville, IN 47129
United States
Tel: +1 812 2848351
Fax: +1 812 2848354
E-mail: info@crisisexperts.com

Critical path analysis

Critical path analysis (CPA) is a beautifully simple method of analysing a complicated task, particularly a business task. It first breaks the task down into a number of discrete jobs (or subtasks). It then finds out which of these subtasks is dependent on others. For example, a car manufacturer cannot put seats into a new car until the car has been painted. The car's engine, however, can be assembled at the same time as the tyres are being manufactured. A restaurant's accounts can be done while its dishes are being washed.

This critical distinction between tasks that can be carried out in parallel and those that have to be carried out in sequence allows the analyst to work out how long the whole task will take; that is, the sum of the time it takes to do all the discrete jobs that have to be carried out in sequence. With this information to hand, it is possible to calculate the resources needed to do all the subtasks. It is also possible to set priorities as to which jobs have to be done first, and thus to determine the sequence in which the jobs must be carried out.

Critical path analysis is often shown in the form of a Gantt chart, a graphic device invented by Henry Gantt, an American consultant who worked closely with Frederick Taylor (see Scientific management, page 193), in the early 20th century. A Gantt chart shows the different subtasks that have to be done as a series of horizontal bars. The horizontal axis of the chart is the time taken. The length of each bar, therefore, represents the time taken by a particular task. Overlapping bars represent tasks that can be done in parallel.

A brief history

Critical path analysis was first developed in the construction industry, where project managers needed to know when to book the plumber, the plasterer, the glazier. It provided them with a continual reminder of how soon the windows could be put in after the walls had been started.

CPA has since been put to more sophisticated uses. It can, for instance, be used to determine a plan of action for the launch of a new product or for an expansion of a firm's manufacturing capacity. In the popular view of the corporation as a value chain (see page 35), it can be a useful tool for deciding how links in the chain might be restructured in order to add yet more value.

Cross-selling

Cross-selling is an idea that became popular in the 1980s and 1990s with the growth of direct selling via the telephone. *The Economist* described it as "the synergistic notion that buyers of one of a firm's services would become customers for another".

Cross-selling involves selling an additional product and service on top of the one that a customer has already agreed to buy or has bought. Its close cousin is up-selling, the idea of upgrading the product that a customer is purchasing to something with extra features or extra services (and extra profit).

A website created by Jim Domanski lays down ten rules for cross-selling and up-selling (www.smartbiz.com/sbs/arts/tor31.htm).

1. **Sell first; tell later.** Do not attempt to up-sell or cross-sell until you have fulfilled the first order. Trying to sell additional items too early can endanger the original sale.
2. **The rule of 25.** The value of any additional sale should not increase the overall order by more than 25%.
3. **Make a profit.** The extra items sold must make enough profit at least to cover the cost of the additional time spent in selling them. But this should not be calculated over a short time frame. Frederick Reichheld, a marketing expert at management consultants Bain & Co, says that most cross-selling fails because companies think only of the next bottom line. They cannot resist trying to sell the highest-margin product rather than the most appropriate one.
4. **Don't dump junk.** Resist the urge to use cross-selling to move unwanted stocks.
5. **Limit and relate.** Limit the add-on items to those that clearly relate to the original purchase. If a customer is buying a blazer from a catalogue, suggesting a shirt and tie makes sense; suggesting a garden hose does not. Much cross-selling of financial services fails because banks try to sell inappropriate products at inappropriate times.
6. **Familiarity breeds success.** The more familiar customers are with the add-on item, the more likely are they to buy it. Cross-selling is not the occasion to introduce a brand new product. Misdirected

marketing at such times can turn clients away in droves.

7 **Plan, plan, plan and plan again.** Decide in advance, for instance, what products each additional item relates to.

8 **Train to avoid pain.** Ensure that the salesman thoroughly understands the products or services being offered.

9 **Test with the best, then roll with the rest.** Test cross-selling first with the best salespeople. They have the drive and initiative to smooth out any of the kinks.

10 **E=MC².** A cross-selling effort (E) is directly dependent on how motivated (M) the salesmen are. Compensation (C) is always a critical factor in selling, as is another C – C for Control.

A brief history

Cross-selling got a bad name when Cendant, a firm that Wall Street had labelled "the growth stock of the universe", fell to earth with a bang in 1998. An accounting fraud of "historic proportions" undermined a company that was built on the skilful cross-selling of a bundle of franchises. These ranged from the Avis car-rental business to the Ramada hotel chain.

Carlson Companies, a huge marketing and travel group, is one of the more successful firms at cross-selling. When Carlson's marketing arm arranges an event for a client (to celebrate an anniversary, say), the group's Carlson Wagonlit travel agents make the necessary bookings for those invited to the event. Many of them then stay in Carlson's Radisson hotels; others take a trip on one of Carlson's luxury cruise ships or eat at one of its TGI Friday restaurants.

Such integrated cross-selling is rare. But it can be hugely profitable.

Recommended reading

Ritter, D.S., *Cross Selling in Financial Services*, John Wiley, 1988
Ritter, D.S., *The Cross Selling Toolkit*, Probus, 1994

Culture

A company's culture is the set of priorities that it gives to different things. Sometimes these priorities are made explicit: in a company's formal mission statement, for example, or in the structure of the organisation and the power given to different departments and functions. Sometimes they are implicit: what the *Financial Times* once called "the large number of unspoken assumptions and beliefs which managers in the organisation share about 'the way we do things around here'".

Edgar Schein of MIT's Sloan School of Management says an organisation's culture is "what it has learned as a total social unit over the course of its history".

Several things shape a corporation's culture.

The employees' behaviour
New recruits in any business usually do what they see, not what they are told. This can range from dress codes to such things as respect for technology and for standard working hours. It can also include the importance given to symbols; for example, to exclusive parking spaces, or to the way that senior managers are addressed, by their first name, or family name, or just by their initials. "Had a good meeting with A.J. this morning. B.J. was there too." Employees' behaviour is also influenced by stories and myths. These record the exploits of legendary leaders of the past, or of famous failures. By the traits that they expose they give strong signals of what is and what is not acceptable; for example, wild alcoholic bingeing or sexual harassment.

The employee selection process
The type of person recruited by an organisation reflects and reinforces its culture. In his book *Inside Organisations*, Charles Handy colourfully described the way that recruits were selected by the Brooke family to help them run the rather large British colony of Sarawak, an area that the family virtually controlled in the years before the second world war.

The first requirement was that:

> ... they had been educated at any of the public schools in
> the West Country [west, that is, of the university town of
> Oxford] – this was the background of the Brooke family and

therefore provided a kind of tribal bonding. Secondly, they must be over six feet tall (the Dyaks, the native people, were small and would, it was thought, be impressed by taller rulers). If they met these conditions they were invited to dinner at the Savoy, given two strong drinks before the meal, wine with it, and two strong drinks after it; if they could then maintain a civilised conversation and walk unfalteringly to the door at the end, they got the job (the Dyaks mixed a powerful drink which local manners required one to drink and remain unaffected by).

Handy went on to say that the Brooke family's case "exemplifies the homogeneous style of organisations in those days". Companies were stuffed with like-minded individuals who exemplified "group think", a recognised condition in which groups of similar people develop a mind-set that is immune to outside influence and the real world.

The nature of the business
Certain industries, such as the movie business or banking, foster a particular culture. New high-technology firms also foster their own (often Silicon Valley influenced) culture. Computer maker Hewlett-Packard, for instance, has for a long time been conscious of its culture (The HP Way) and has worked hard to maintain it over the years through extensive training. Hewlett-Packard's culture is based on respect for others, a sense of community and plain old hard work (according to *Fortune Magazine*, May 15th 1995).

The external environment
Companies need to take into account the culture of the society in which they are operating. American multinationals, for instance, cannot transpose the methods of Milwaukee straight into downtown Mombasa and expect to have a harmonious operation.

One of the few areas of management study that has been dominated by Europeans rather than Americans is cross-cultural management. Europeans have a natural advantage. Fons Trompenaars, an authority in the field, once wrote that his Dutch father and his French mother gave him "an understanding of the fact that if something works in one culture, there is little chance that it will work in another".

Geert Hofstede, a long respected figure in the area, is a Dutch academic who also spent long periods in industry, most notably at IBM. He also founded the Institute for Research on International Co-operation. Hofstede's work has provided a framework for understanding cultural differences. The Hofstede Cultural Orientation Model is based on a study of the employees of one multinational company in 40 different countries, and it classifies cultures along five different dimensions.

1 **Individual versus collective.** This refers to the extent to which individuals expect only to look after themselves and their immediate families, compared with the extent to which there is a tight social framework in which people expect the groups to which they belong to look after them. In exchange for the care of the group, they give their absolute loyalty.

   This distinction has been most extensively examined in the context of the United States and Japan. Japan's excellent industrial performance has sometimes been credited to the propensity of the Japanese to work in groups. An American writer, Richard Pascale, however, has warned of the risks of assuming that culture is ever the dominant explanatory variable of superior industrial performance. Soon after the worship of Japanese collectivism came to an end with the spluttering of the Japanese economy in the 1990s, American individuality and the entrepreneurial spirit came back into fashion.

2 **Power distance.** This refers to the extent to which a society accepts the fact that power in institutions and organisations is distributed unequally.

3 **Uncertainty avoidance.** This is the extent to which employees feel threatened by ambiguity, and the relative importance that they attach to rules, long-term employment and steady progression up a well-defined career ladder.

4 **Masculinity.** This refers to the nature of the dominant values in the organisation. For example, is the organisation dominated by masculine values such as assertiveness and monetary focus, rather than feminine values such as concern for others and the quality of relationships?

5 **Short term versus long term.** This refers to the different time frames used by different people and organisations. Those with a short-term view are more inclined towards consumption and to maintaining face by keeping up with the neighbours. With a long-term attitude the focus is on preserving status-based relationships and on thrift.

A brief history

The management of corporate culture became a hot issue in the late 20th century. But it is far from being a new issue. As long ago as 1527, the unusually perceptive Niccolo Machiavelli had something to say about it:

> *When a conqueror acquires states in a province which is different from his own in language, customs and institutions, great difficulties arise, and excellent fortune and great skill are needed to retain them.*

Machiavelli hit upon the two things that brought about the 1990s revival of interest in the subject.

- **Globalisation.** The princes of the business world were spreading their affairs more widely than ever before. The growth of joint ventures and of cross-border partnerships put more and more businesses under pressure to work productively with people from a wide variety of ethnic backgrounds and cultures. The arrival of the Disney culture in France in the 1990s was a notorious case of culture clash. So ill-attuned to the differences in Europe was the Disney organisation that at one stage the operation almost had to be closed down.

- **Mergers and acquisitions.** The princes were also devouring new businesses at a rate that made Machiavelli's masters, the Borgia family, look like anorexics. Many mergers and acquisitions brought together two or more companies of very different cultures and then expected them to be more productive than they were as independent fiefdoms. Cultural differences are often cited as the single greatest impediment to making mergers work.

Some companies build up their culture through training. Others strengthen it by having a clearly written mission statement. One of the most extraordinary was that drawn up by Marks & Spencer, a British retailer. Its mission, it said, was:

> *The subversion of the class structure of 19th century England by making available to the working and lower-middle classes, upper-class quality at prices the working and lower-middle classes could well afford.*

Some companies go beyond mission statements and into vision statements. These are intended to lay out some ideal future state of the company.

Recommended reading

Coupland, D., *Microserfs*, HarperCollins, 1996

Hofstede, G., *Cultures and Organisations: Software of the Mind*, McGraw-Hill, 1991

Johnson, G., "Strategy, Culture and Managerial Action", *Long Range Planning Journal*, February 1992

Morosini, P., *Managing Cultural Differences*, Pergamon, 1998

Pascale, R., "Communication and Decision-Making Across Cultures: Japanese and American Comparisons", *Administrative Science Quarterly*, Vol. 23, 1978

Schein, E., *Organisational Culture and Leadership*, Jossey-Bass, 1985

Trompenaars, F. and Hampden-Turner, C., *Riding the Waves of Culture*, Nicholas Brealey, 1993

Watson, T., *A Business and its Beliefs: the Ideas that Helped Build IBM*, McGraw-Hill, 1963

Customer relationship management

Customer relationship management, commonly known as CRM, is part of a late 20th-century systematic shift in the structure and strategies of corporations. It is, says Dale Renner, managing partner for CRM at Andersen Consulting, something that encompasses "identifying, attracting and retaining the most valuable customers to sustain profitable growth."

CRM is a way of designing structures and systems so that the company is focused on providing consumers (profitably) with what they want, rather than on making products that it, the company, thinks they might want. In particular, it involves a restructuring of the company's information technology systems and a reorganisation of its staff. It is heavily dependent on a technique called data warehousing, a way of integrating disparate information about customers from different parts of the organisation and putting it together in one huge IT "warehouse". With data warehousing, for example, any employee who enters a customer's name into the central computer comes up with details of all the transactions that have been carried out with that customer.

This is contrary to the product-oriented way in which most firms grew up, when divisions and business units were built around products and product groups. It was not then unusual for each group to have its own accounts department, its own IT unit and its own marketing team. People who worked for these vertically integrated silos were often competing as much against other silos within the same organisation as against outside rivals in the market place. Their loyalty to their silo frequently blinded them to the wider interests of the company as a whole.

CRM is about putting structures and systems in place that cut across the vertical lines of the traditional firm and focus on individual customers. With vertical silos, customers could be approached by the same firm in several different product guises over a short period of time. No one bit of the firm would know what any other bit was doing at any particular time.

A brief history

The phrase "the customer is king" was first coined long before it was true. Only towards the end of the 20th century, when advances in technology and widespread market deregulation put enormous new power into the hands of consumers, did it stop sounding hollow.

Two things in particular brought home to companies the need to make themselves more customer-oriented. First, some terrible mistakes were made because of the blinkers imposed by the old product-silo approach. For example, market share was the goal and the yardstick of such structures. Yet when IBM was king of the mainframe computer market, it understood just in time that 100% of a market that was rapidly disappearing would soon be 100% of nothing.

IBM realised that instead of focusing on the mainframe computer market, it should have been focusing on what its customers really wanted. This was not mainframe computers as such, but rather the power to process information electronically. Academics have called this different concept of a market "a market space". Children's playtime is a market space. A doll is a product, an object.

The second thing that drove companies to focus more closely on their customers was a growing awareness that building up profits by aggregating narrow margins from the sale of individual products might not be the best way of ensuring the long-term health of the corporation. Companies that did this would always be vulnerable either to cherry-pickers (see page 31), firms that were happy to slice their margins even more thinly for the sake of rapid growth in market share, or to nimble newcomers that were able to work off a different cost base, made possible by deregulation or by changing distribution channels.

Motor-cycle manufacturer Harley-Davidson is one company that went through a process of CRM and got rid of its old vertical organisation. In its place it chose a structure in which three circles of influence overlap at the centre. The circles – called the Create Demand Circle, the Produce Products Circle and the Support Circle – were designed to emphasise collaboration and to avoid giving the customer the idea that the right hand did not know what the left hand was up to.

Such horizontal restructurings invariably arouse fears of job losses among the workforce. But Xerox, a much larger company than Harley-Davidson, went through a similar restructuring and did not eliminate a single job during the process. Instead of cutting jobs it redefined them.

More companies are coming to regard their customers as customers for life and not just as the one-off purchasers of a product. It is common knowledge that it is far less expensive to retain an existing customer than it is to acquire a new one. So, companies ask, why not try to serve the same customers throughout their life, to fill their shifting market spaces from youth through to old age? In this framework it becomes important for companies to measure their customers' lifetime value, and to think about cross-subsidising different periods of their lives. Banks make little or no money out of their student customers, for example, in the hope that they will become more valuable in their later years.

Recommended reading

Kotler, P., *Managing Customer Relationships: Lessons from the Leaders*, The Economist Intelligence Unit, 1998

Peppers, D. and Rogers, M., *The One-to-One Manager*, Doubleday, 1999

Vandermerwe, S., *The Eleventh Commandment, Transforming to Own Customers*, John Wiley, 1996

Decentralisation

Decentralisation is the process of distributing power away from the centre of an organisation. In the case of a corporation this means divesting authority away from the head office and outwards to operators in the field. Debate centres on which is the more efficient structure for an organisation that has a number of far-flung arms, especially a multinational with operations in a number of different countries: one where decision-making is concentrated at the centre, or one where it is diffused around the organisation?

Decentralisation and its alter ego, centralisation, have been fashionable in phases. In his famous-for-its-title book, *Small is Beautiful* (see page 200), E.F. Schumacher wrote:

> *Once a large organisation has come into being, it normally*
> *goes through alternating phases of centralising and*
> *decentralising, like swings of a pendulum. Whenever one*
> *encounters such opposites, each of them with persuasive*
> *arguments in its favour, it is worth looking into the depth of*
> *the problem for something more than compromise, more*
> *than a half-and-half solution. Maybe what we really need is*
> *not either/or but "the one and the other at the same time".*
> *This very familiar problem pervades the whole of real life.*

Other famous management writers have been less equivocal. In a classic book by Alfred Chandler, *Strategy and Structure*, the author argued that strategy was the responsibility of head office, but day-to-day operations should be left to decentralised units.

Tom Peters, co-author with Robert Waterman of *In Search of Excellence*, recounts how in the mid-1990s he and Waterman were each asked separately to list the big challenges facing business. He says:

> *The lists bore little resemblance to one another – except for*
> *the first item. Both of us put ... decentralisation at the top of*
> *our lists ... after 50 (combined) years of watching*
> *organisations thrive and shrivel, we held to one, and only*
> *one, basic belief: to loosen the reins, to allow a thousand*
> *flowers to bloom and a hundred schools to contend, is the*

best way to sustain vigour in perilous gyrating times.

A brief history

Decentralisation has had its supporters for centuries. In the 1700s, the East India Company was a highly decentralised organisation, but only because it had no other option. Its factors ran its factories in remote parts of the world. There was no telegraph, telephone or telex. They had to make decisions for themselves there and then.

Just as the state of technology determined the degree of centralisation for the East India Company, so it had a dramatic effect on subsequent enthusiasm for the idea. Decentralisation remained the dominant model for most of the 19th century. The Morgans, father and son, ran their banks in isolated independence in London and New York, and the various arms of the Rothschild family ran their banks independently in a number of European countries. Carrier pigeon was the fastest form of communication that they could hope for.

With the invention of the telephone and the telex, the head office came into its own, and throughout most of the 20th century centralisation was the dominant philosophy. It was a shift brought about for the most part by Alexander Graham Bell.

There were exceptions, of course. The American chemicals company DuPont enthusiastically embraced the idea of decentralisation in the mid-1920s when its senior executives developed a multidivisional structure to cope with the company's diversification. Likewise, Alfred Sloan split General Motors into divisions, and each division was run as a company within a company. Sloan said the company was "co-ordinated in policy and decentralised in administration". It was a move that helped him to claw back some of the enormous advantage that Ford had gained from its introduction a decade earlier of mass production and the assembly line.

In the 1990s the growth and rapid development of information technology began to turn the tables. The Internet and other electronic information systems made the distribution of information ubiquitous and cheap. Power was once again diffused outwards to workers in the field. In an article in the *Harvard Business Review* in 1998, C.K. Prahalad and Kenneth Lieberthal argued that this diffusion of power would have a particularly powerful impact on multinationals. The old imperialist assumption that all innovation comes from the centre will no longer be valid. Innovation will have to be encouraged locally, and locally recruited employees will have to be able to rise to the top of the organisation.

Recommended reading

Chandler, A., *Strategy and Structure*, Doubleday-Anchor, 1966

Prahalad, C.K. and Lieberthal, K., "The End of Corporate Imperialism", *Harvard Business Review*, July-August 1998

Sloan, A.P., *My Years with General Motors*, Doubleday, 1954

Delayering

Delayering involves reducing the number of levels in an organisation's hierarchy. Classically, this has meant reducing the dozen or so layers that were typical of the large corporation of the 1950s to the five or so layers that by the end of the century were deemed to be the maximum with which any large organisation could function effectively.

Delayering is not just a way of stripping out jobs and cutting overheads. It usually involves increasing the average span of control (see page 202) of the senior managers within the organisation. This can, in effect, chop the number of layers without removing a single name from the payroll.

Delayering is a radical redesign of an organisation's structure to take account of late 20th-century developments in information technology, education and consumer demand. Essentially, it involves a flattening of the organisation from a giant pyramid to something more horizontal. It is not an anarchic denial of the need for structure.

Frank Ostroff's book *The Horizontal Organisation* reflects late 20th-century thinking about organisational structure. In it he writes:

> *Structure is still critical to designing an efficient organisation for the 21st or any other century, and certain essential points must be considered: Who goes where? What do they do? What are the positions and how are they grouped? What is the reporting sequence? What is each person accountable for? In other words, how does the authority flow?*

In yet other words, how do the organisation's layers lie?

Among the benefits claimed for the delayered organisation are the following.

- It needs fewer managers.
- It is less bureaucratic.
- It can take decisions more quickly.
- It encourages innovation.
- It brings managers into closer contact with the organisation's customers.

◪ It produces cross-functional employees.

This is not easy to achieve, and delayering efforts often stumble. A common cause is failure to include a sufficiently sensitive reappraisal of the changed rewards that must go with redesigned jobs.

A brief history

Companies such as AT&T, General Electric, Motorola and Xerox were at the forefront of delayering, creating horizontal organisations that were built around core processes, not functions. Paul Allaire, chairman of Xerox at the time it "went horizontal", says that before the change:

> [The company was] functional in nature. So every function –
> sales, service, administrative, manufacturing, engineering,
> research and development – all came up the line and, in the
> end, reported to me. Short of ordering office supplies and
> conducting minor day-to-day activities, I was the only one
> responsible for anything in its entirety.

Xerox moved from that form to a structure based on work flows and the value chain. Functional silos were dismantled and cross-functional teams were put together to carry out the work that Xerox's customers were prepared to pay for.

Recommended reading

Ashkenas, R., Ulrich, D., Jink, T. and Kerr, S., The Boundaryless
    Organization, Jossey Bass, 1995
Austin, N., "Flattening the Pyramid", Incentive, December 1993
Krackhardt, D. and Hanson, J.R., "Informal Networks: The Company
    Behind the Chart", Harvard Business Review, July-August 1993
Ostroff, F. and Smith, D., "The Horizontal Organization", McKinsey
    Quarterly, No. 1, 1992
Ostroff, F., The Horizontal Organisation, Oxford University Press, 1999

Differentiation

The concept of differentiation originated in economics and has been taken over by marketing departments. At its heart lies the ability of similar products to be differentiated by real or imaginary means, thus enabling them to be sold at a higher price and profit. This differentiation can take real forms (soluble aspirin as against non-soluble aspirin, for example) or imaginary forms (by advertising that suggests one perfume makes you more attractive to the opposite sex than another).

The value of differentiation increases the more that products come to resemble each other. For example, washing machines and airline flights vary less and less as time goes by, and it becomes a bigger and bigger challenge to differentiate one from another. Once a distinction has been established, however, it can be reaffirmed for years and years. Porsche, for example, differentiates itself as being a fast-moving sports car for fast-moving high-fliers, and has done at least since James Dean, a film actor, happened to die in one in 1956.

In consumer-goods industries it is common for a large number of differentiated products to be produced by quite a small number of firms. For example, most of the seemingly wide range of soaps and detergents in the United States are produced by just two firms, Unilever and Procter & Gamble. In commodity markets, such as oil and coal, there is little or no scope for differentiation. These industries also have low returns on investment. In industries where there is scope for differentiation, there is a far wider range of returns.

Service businesses differentiate themselves in different ways from manufacturers. Airlines rely both on their products ("our fleet is newer than blah blahs") and on their personnel ("our flight attendants are prettier and more attentive"). This does not work with products ("our chickens have been plucked by people with cleaner hands").

Brand image is another way of differentiating products. This is particularly powerful in the fashion industry, where it is hard to argue that "our clothes last longer than xxx's" or that "we have better taste than xxx". It is also significant in the tobacco industry, where one cigarette is so much like another.

Marketers maintain that most products can be differentiated in some way. Philip Kotler, a marketing guru, gives the example of the brick industry, which is about as close to a commodity business as it is possible to be. Yet one company in the industry was able to differentiate itself dramatically by altering its method of delivering bricks. Instead of dumping them on the ground (and breaking a bundle), it stacked them together on pallets and used a small crane to lift them gently off the truck. So successful was the firm with this method that before long it became standard industry practice. The firm then, of course, had to look for a new way of differentiating itself.

A brief history

In Michael Porter's ground-breaking work on the competition of the firm (see Competitive advantage, page 35) he argued that there are only two ways for firms to compete: on price, or by differentiating their products from those of their rivals.

This focused attention on product differentiation as a marketing strategy designed to make consumers aware of the differences between one company's product and everyone else's. (See also Unique selling proposition, page 229.) Advertising could then be introduced to emphasise how these differences made a product better value for money and, therefore, the one to buy.

Recommended reading

Beath, J. and Katsoulacos, Y., *The Economic Theory of Product Differentiation*, Cambridge University Press, 1991

Kotler, P. and Armstrong, G., *Principles of Marketing*, Prentice Hall (8th edition), 1999

Ries, A. and Trout, J., *Positioning: the Battle for your Mind*, McGraw-Hill, 1981

Ries, A. and Trout, J., *Marketing Warfare*, McGraw-Hill, 1986

Smith, W.R., "Product Differentiation and Market Segmentation as Alternative Marketing Strategies", *Journal of Marketing*, July 1956

Trout, J., *Differentiate or Die*, John Wiley, 2000

Diversification

From time to time companies become nervous about putting all their commercial eggs into one basket. Their heads are turned by the portfolio theory of investment, in which exposure to risk is reduced through the ownership of a wide range of shares. So they set out to do the same – to reduce the risk from being in too few businesses by getting into more of them. They do this either by buying businesses or by starting them up internally from scratch, the former being the more common. Companies that follow this strategy of diversification have a name. They are called conglomerates.

Conglomerates take some of the job of spreading risk out of the hands of shareholders and put it into the hands of corporate managers. Shareholders can choose to buy either a diversified portfolio of shares, or a share with a diversified portfolio.

Although conglomerates come in and out of fashion, there are timeless reasons in favour of diversification. It can give rise to opportunities to share overheads or to exploit synergies (see page 218). Firms can make savings by selling a wider range of goods with the same infrastructure. Department stores profitably sell everything from armchairs to underwear. The same logic can be applied to manufacturers of armchairs and underwear.

Diversification has proved to be a highly successful strategy for some large companies. Constantinos Markides, a professor at the London Business School, says that the rewards and risks can be extraordinary. He quotes success stories such as General Electric, Disney and 3M, but also mentions notorious failures, such as Quaker Oats's doomed entry into the fruit juice business through a company called Snapple, and Blue Circle, a British cement producer, which diversified into making lawn mowers on no firmer grounds, according to one former executive of the company, than that "your garden is next to your house".

A brief history

The idea of diversification was given a big boost by a book called *Portfolio Selection*, published in the late 1950s. It urged investors (individual and corporate) to spread their risks by spreading their investments. Around 1952 a company called Royal Little had shown the way, acquiring companies in unrelated industries while maintaining steady growth.

Enthusiasm for diversification was particularly high in the 1960s and early 1970s. Between 1960 and 1980, the percentage of the Fortune 500 leading American companies that could be described as conglomerates rose from 50 to 80. The prototype was ITT. Under Harold Geneen, an Englishman who headed the American company for many years, ITT simultaneously owned bakeries, telephone companies, hotels and a forest-products business. In the early 1970s it had over 400 separate subsidiaries operating in over 70 different countries.

Diversification went out of fashion in the 1980s and 1990s, however, when companies began to see again the virtues of "sticking to their knitting". Many shed businesses that they had bought only a few years before in their headlong rush to be a conglomerate. Exxon rapidly withdrew from the electronics business, for example, and BP retreated from coal. CBS, an American broadcaster, is reckoned to have sold off more than 80% of its portfolio of businesses, and P&O sold off a wide range of businesses in order to refocus on shipping, especially the cruise business.

Markides believes that companies miss significant opportunities when they reject diversification as a strategic option. A role model for the late 20th-century conglomerate is the Canadian firm Bombardier. Founded in 1942 as a manufacturer of snow-going equipment, it grew rapidly in the last quarter of the century to become a diversified manufacturer of products ranging from mass-transit systems to personal watercraft. By the end of the century it had manufacturing facilities in nine countries and some 40,000 employees. In 1997 the company's chief executive explained its strategy:

> Bombardier never diversified at breakneck speed. The first
> move, entering the mass-transit equipment industry,
> occurred in 1974; the second step, acquiring Canadair, was
> taken 12 years later. After each initial foray into a new
> industry, we made a series of acquisitions within it to
> strengthen our position. [Moreover,] each new sector we
> entered shares certain fundamental similarities in terms of
> key manufacturing processes, procurement, engineering
> design, and product development.

Recommended reading
Geneen, H. (with Moscow, A.), Managing, Doubleday, 1984
Markides, C., "To Diversify or Not to Diversify", Harvard Business
Review, November-December 1997

Markowitz, H.M., *Portfolio Selection*, John Wiley, 1959

Salter, M.S. and Porter, M., "Note on Diversification as Strategy", *Harvard Business Review*, November-December 1986

Utton, M.A., *Diversification and Competition*, Cambridge University Press, 1979

Double-loop learning

The idea of double-loop learning is difficult to grasp, but it has been sufficiently powerful to become central to much discussion about the way in which organisations learn (see Learning organisation, page 138). It was first developed by a Harvard professor of organisational behaviour, Chris Argyris, in the 1970s. Argyris contrasted double-loop learning with single-loop learning, and described the distinction between them in several different ways and on several different occasions.

In one article he wrote:

> When a thermostat turns the heat on or off, it is acting in keeping with the program of orders given to it to keep the room temperature, let us say, at 68 degrees. This is single-loop learning, because the underlying program is not questioned.

Double-loop learning would require the thermostat not only to adjust the temperature but also to question why it was set at 68 degrees in the first place.

Argyris said in another context:

> The overwhelming amount of learning done in an organisation is single loop because it is designed to identify and correct errors so that the job gets done and the action remains within stated policy guidelines.

In double-loop learning, executives continually question the policies and objectives within which their decision-making power is constrained.

Single-loop learning is dangerous because it confirms stereotypes. "The theory-in-use is self-fulfilling." Argyris gives the example of a manager who believes his subordinates are passive and dependent on guidance. Such a manager tests his belief by giving his subordinates challenges that confirm his theory. To get out of this "single loop" the manager has to engage in "open-loop learning", where he deliberately tries to disprove the generally held theory. He has to ask what it would take to show that his subordinates were not dependent on guidance.

Double-loop learning is difficult because most individuals are unaware of their reasoning processes, of the implicit rules underlying the decisions that they take. Argyris says there are two reasons for this:

> First, they have great reasoning skill – the activity is second nature to them and they are rarely aware of it while they are doing it. Indeed, as is true of most skilled behaviour, they rarely focus on it unless they make an error. Second, when they do make errors, other people – especially subordinates – may feel it is safest to play down the error, or they may ease in the correct information so subtly that the executive will probably not even realise that he did make an error.

A brief history

Examples of companies that have expensively failed to question the underlying assumptions behind a particular management theory include the Japanese electronics firm Sony. When it introduced the Walkman, it followed a brilliantly successful strategy of allowing the market to decide which of a wide range of variations on the theme it preferred. It then used its skill in getting new products rapidly to market to meet the expressed demand. However, when it tried to implement the same strategy (of making many variants on a single theme) with video it did not work. The company lost billions of dollars learning something that it should have picked up (if it had been applying double-loop learning) the first time that it tried the strategy.

Recommended reading

Argyris, C. and Schon, D., *Theory in Practice: Increasing Professional Effectiveness*, Jossey Bass, 1974
Argyris, C., *Increasing Leadership Effectiveness*, John Wiley, 1976
Argyris, C., "Double Loop Learning in Organisations", *Harvard Business Review*, January-February 1977

Downsizing

Downsizing, its supporters insist, is not primarily about job cuts. It is, they say, a process whereby a corporation adjusts to changed market circumstances. It is not just what companies do when they hit a recession. Although downsizing implies a reduction in assets, it is not merely a reduction in the human assets.

Other terms have been used to distance the concept from its association with ruthless job-slashing – for example, rightsizing and restructuring. In the first IBM annual report after his appointment as chief executive of the huge computer company, Lou Gerstner said, "Shortly after I joined, I set as my highest priority to rightsize the company as quickly as we could."

The downsizing of corporate staff was at its most intense in the late 1980s and early 1990s. In the United States alone, some 3.5m workers lost their jobs to downsizing in the decade after 1987. The losses had much to do with getting rid of layers of middle managers – a move made necessary by increasing competition and the growth of an information technology which reduced the need for human ciphers.

Some saw it as marking a return to organisational structures of long ago. In a 1988 article in the *Harvard Business Review*, Peter Drucker wrote that one of the best examples of a large and successful information-based organisation that had no middle management at all was the British civil administration in India. The Indian civil service never had more than 1,000 members, most of whom were under 30 years of age. Each political secretary (a senior rank) had at least 100 people reporting directly to him, "many times what the doctrine of the span of control [see page 202] would allow". It worked, added Drucker, "in large part because it was designed to ensure that each of its members had the information he needed to do his job".

A brief history

By the late 1990s there was a reaction against downsizing. Companies started asking themselves whether it had all gone too far. By then they knew that there was a considerable downside to downsizing. First, it left organisations shell-shocked and demoralised. Those who had job options resigned, and their employer was then frequently forced to rehire in what has been described as a process of "binge and purge". The short-term benefits to the bottom line from downsizing could be offset by the long-term damage to the loyalty, morale and (possibly) the productivity of those employees who did stay.

In 1995, the American Management Association (AMA) surveyed 1,000 companies on the effects of downsizing. Only 48% of those that had cut jobs since 1990 said that their profits went up afterwards. The AMA survey also found that downsizing failed to improve product quality at most of these companies.

In a special report on the changing structure of the workplace published in October 1994, *Business Week* magazine warned that the great risk of downsizing was that it simply resulted in fewer people working harder. It did little to change the way that work was done within the corporation. A middle manager at a high-tech company recounted his experience:

> *This year, I had to downsize my area by 25%. Nothing
> changed in terms of the workload. It's very emotionally
> draining. I find myself not wanting to go in to work,
> because I'm going to have to push people to do more, and I
> look at their eyes and they're sinking into the back of their
> heads. But they're not going to complain, because they don't
> want to be the next 25%.*

Another apparent downside to downsizing is the loss of a company's innovative ability. According to Deborah Dougherty of McGill University and Edward Bowman of the University of Pennsylvania's Wharton School, downsized firms lose the ability to carry out a crucial final stage in the process of bringing a new product to market. Downsizing interferes with the network of informal relationships which innovators use to gain support for new product development. Innovative activities no longer connect with the rest of the firm.

The caring company's alternative to downsizing is reallocation. If jobs have to go, it does not mean that employees have to go as well. 3M's policy, for example, is to find similar jobs for excess workers in other divisions. During the 1990s it reassigned 3,500 workers in this way rather than make them redundant. It is able to do this because it is constantly creating new products and new divisions to which these people can be relocated.

Recommended reading

Allen, J.G., *Surviving Corporate Downsizing*, John Wiley, 1988
Drucker, P., "The Coming of The New Organisation" *Harvard Business Review*, Vol. 66, No. 1, 1988
Hamill, J., "Employment Effects of Changing Multinational Strategies in Europe", *European Management Journal*, Vol. 10, No. 3
www.csaf.org/downsize.htm – Making sense of corporate downsizing
www.ilr.cornell.edu/library/books...nsizing/GAO-downsizing.htmt – Workforce reduction: Downsizing strategies used in selected organisations

E-commerce

The term e-commerce embraces all the ways of transacting business via electronic data: for example, the Minitel system in France, videotext systems, and direct selling by phone. But it is most closely identified with commerce transacted over the Internet, and it is the Internet that has put e-commerce at the head of the corporate strategic agenda for the first years of the 21st century.

E-commerce is merely an elision of electronic commerce, but it embodies a revolutionary idea: that electronic commerce is qualitatively different from ordinary time-worn commerce, that (in the jargon) there is a paradigm shift in the way that business is conducted in the world of e-commerce. Conducting business via the Internet is not only much quicker and much cheaper than other methods, it is also thought to overturn old rules about time, space and price. There is the much-vaunted death of distance: a customer 10,000 miles away becomes as accessible as one around the corner.

Furthermore, economies of scale, economic laws that were assumed for centuries to be immutable, become irrelevant. A newspaper like the *Wall Street Journal*, for example, sells its online edition for a fraction of the price of its paper-based edition. There is no difference in its unit delivery cost if it sells five or 5,000 online copies. This is a revolution for organisations whose structures and strategies have built-in assumptions about relationships between price and volume.

A brief history

Electronic commerce grew rapidly in the late 1990s. Forrester Research, an American research company whose figures on the subject are the most widely quoted, says that business-to-business e-commerce in 1998 amounted to $43 billion. The company estimated that it would double every year for the next five years and reach $1.3 billion by 2003. Forrester also estimated that direct business-to-consumer e-commerce would grow at a more modest rate, rising from $8 billion in 1998 to $108 billion by 2003. Measuring these things, however, is a tricky business.

Companies like Dell Computer made extraordinary cost savings through early use of the Internet to sell goods and services direct to consumers, and to buy components from their suppliers. Financial-service offerings over the Internet sprouted like mushrooms. At American retail brokerage firm Charles Schwab, for instance, online dealing came to account for more than half of all its securities trading in just three years.

For banks, however, e-commerce presented both an opportunity and a threat. It has been estimated that a banking transaction carried out over the telephone costs half as much as the same transaction conducted over the counter in a traditional branch, and an ATM transaction costs a quarter as much. But a banking transaction over the Internet costs a mere 1% of an over-the-counter transaction at a branch. This presents established banks with an opportunity to turn their cost structure upside down if they can persuade customers to do their banking online and to stop queuing at branches.

However, it also allows unknown firms to establish new businesses cheaply and rapidly, and to compete with the old-timers. They do this not only by cutting prices and offering wider choices, but also by allowing consumers to make real-time price comparisons (via electronic marketplaces like Annuity.net) and to switch rapidly (and frequently) to the cheapest provider (via electronic transfer systems like OneSource).

The world's major stockmarkets took to e-commerce with enthusiasm. America Online, an early Internet service provider, was rapidly valued at more than General Motors and went on to buy Netscape, a pioneering Internet company, and to merge with TimeWarner. But some observers of the e-commerce scene cannot see how such firms will ever make exceptional profits. It is fundamental to e-commerce that the customer is in control. Customers can search the web rapidly and ruthlessly to seek out the cheapest price. E-commerce, these observers claim, is a business of, at best, low margins and, at worst, no margins.

Recommended reading

Baldock, R., *Destination Z*, John Wiley, 1998
"Business and the Internet", survey by *The Economist*, June 26th 1999

Economies of scale

Economies of scale are those factors that cause the average cost of producing something to fall as the volume of its output increases. Hence it might cost $3,000 to produce 100 copies of a magazine but only $4,000 to produce 1,000 copies. The average cost in this case has fallen from $30 to $4 a copy because the main elements of cost in producing a magazine are loaded at the front end of the production process.

Economies of scale were the main drivers of corporate gigantism in the 20th century. They were fundamental to Henry Ford's revolutionary assembly line (see Mass production, page 148), and they are the spur to most mergers and acquisitions today.

There are two types of economies of scale.

◪ **Internal.** Cost savings that accrue to a firm regardless of the industry, market or environment in which it operates.
◪ **External.** Economies that benefit a firm as a result of the way in which its industry is organised.

Internal economies of scale can arise in a number of areas. For example, it is easier for large firms to carry the overheads of sophisticated research and development (R&D). In the pharmaceuticals industry R&D is vital. Yet the cost of discovering the next blockbuster drug is enormous and increasing. Several of the mergers between pharmaceuticals companies in recent years have been driven by little more than such companies' desire to spread their R&D expenditure across a greater volume of sales.

Internal economies of scale can also arise from spreading the high fixed costs of plant and machinery across a larger volume of sales. Electric power generation and steel manufacture are two industries where a sizeable critical mass of turnover is required before any initial capital investment in plant and machinery can be justified. They are not businesses for the small at heart.

Large firms also gain internal economies of scale because they are able to use specialised labour and machinery more efficiently than small firms. A large firm's complicated assembly line and its specialist workers are less likely to be left expensively idle than those of a small firm.

However, economies of scale have a dark side, and this is called diseconomies of scale. The larger an organisation becomes in order to reap economies of scale, the more complex it has to become to manage and run such scale. This complexity incurs a cost. Eventually, this cost may come to outweigh the savings to be gained from greater scale. In other words, economies of scale cannot be gleaned for ever.

Frederick Herzberg, a distinguished professor of management, suggested another reason that companies should not aim blindly for economies of scale:

> Numbers numb our feelings for what is being counted and lead to adoration of the economies of scale. Passion is in feeling, the quality of experience, not in trying to measure it.

T. Boone Pickens, a geologist turned oil magnate turned corporate raider, wrote about diseconomies of scale in his 1987 autobiography:

> It's unusual to find a large corporation that's efficient. I know about economies of scale and all the other advantages that are supposed to come with size. But when you get an inside look, it's easy to see how inefficient big business really is. Most corporate bureaucracies have more people than they have work. Large corporations were great at setting up massive assembly lines, but terrible at modifying those same lines to fit changing conditions.

The big advantage of being big used to be that it allowed a company to buy inputs more cheaply the more that it bought. But today the Internet can, in many cases, undermine economies of scale.

In its April 1999 report "Making Open Finance Pay", Forrester Research gave examples of the way in which the Internet has altered the pricing structure of a number of industries, particularly those with a high information content. Before the advent of the Internet it cost $100 to make an equity market order. Afterwards it cost just $15, an 85% fall in price, far more than could ever have been gleaned from traditional economies of scale.

Recommended reading

Sloan, A.P., *My Years with General Motors*, Doubleday, 1954
Smith, A., *The Wealth of Nations*, 1776

Economies of scope

Economies of scope are those factors that make it cheaper to produce a range of products together than to produce each one of them on its own. These economies can come from businesses sharing centralised functions, such as finance or marketing. Or they can come from interrelationships elsewhere in the business process, such as cross-selling one product alongside another, or using the outputs of one business as the inputs of another.

Just as the economic theory of economies of scale (see page 76) has been the underpinning for all sorts of corporate behaviour, from mass production to mergers and acquisitions, so the theory of economies of scope has been the underpinning for a different sort of corporate behaviour, particularly for diversification (see page 66).

A brief history

The desire to garner economies of scope was the driving force behind the creation of vast international conglomerates in the 1970s and 1980s, including BTR and Hanson in the UK and ITT in the United States. The logic behind these amalgamations lay mostly in the scope for the companies to leverage their financial skills across a diversified range of industries.

Hanson was a classic example of a company that grew in this way. In the early 1960s it was a small family haulage business based in Yorkshire. By the early 1990s it was the UK's fourth largest manufacturer, making batteries, typewriters, bricks, HP sauce and Jacuzzi whirlpool baths after a riot of mergers and acquisitions in both the UK and the United States. Its growth, however, depended on it being able to add shareholder value by making bigger and bigger acquisitions. As with much other industrial diversification, there turned out to be little synergy to be gained from making batteries and bricks under one roof. In the end, the only economies of scope came from sharing a narrow range of head office skills and a chief executive.

By the 1990s industrial conglomerates had fallen out of favour. There was little enthusiasm for economies of scope that (it transpired) depended on making ever larger acquisitions of yet more unrelated industries. Hanson, BTR, ITT and others became shadows of their former selves.

A number of conglomerates in the 1990s, however, were put together in a burst of enthusiasm for cross-selling (see page 49), reaping economies of scope from using the same people and systems to sell many products. Companies like the American group Cendant excited the stockmarket with the promise of synergies to come from (in its case) selling hotel rooms, insurance and car-rentals from under one roof. The massive combination of Travelers Group and Citicorp in 1998 was based on producing big cost savings from cross-selling the financial products of one by the sales teams of the other.

Empowerment

Empowerment is the idea that an organisation is most productive when all its employees are empowered to make and take decisions, when authority is devolved down to all levels of the organisation. It is a feel-good idea that seems to prove what all sensitive, progressive people know should be the case. The idea was most closely associated with Rosabeth Moss Kanter, a Harvard Business School professor who also edited the *Harvard Business Review*, and it was central to her influential book *When Giants Learn to Dance*.

Kanter argued that large companies need to liberate their employees from stultifying hierarchies if they are going to be able to "dance" in the flexible, fast-changing future. Too many employees, she believed, still needed "the crutch" of hierarchy. These "powerless" people, said Kanter, "live in a different world ... they may turn instead to the ultimate weapon of those who lack productive power – oppressive power". She felt that women were particularly in need of empowerment because traditionally they had been employed in low-status jobs.

The idea harks back to Douglas McGregor's Theory X and Theory Y (see page 223). It gives McGregor's framework a new spin by adding information technology. IT has the ability to put into the hands of Theory Y'ers (self-motivating individuals) the raw material (knowledge, or power) that they need in order to act responsibly and to take decisions for themselves.

A brief history

Ten years after Kanter's book, another Harvard Business School professor, Chris Argyris, wrote an article in the *Harvard Business Review* entitled "Empowerment: The Emperor's New Clothes". It said, more or less, "Nice idea; shame about the results". Everyone talks about empowerment, said Argyris, but it is not working. Chief executives subtly undermine it, despite Kanter's assertion that "by empowering others, a leader does not decrease his power". Employees are often unprepared or unwilling to assume the new responsibilities that it entails.

To find out why it was not working, Argyris set empowerment in the context of commitment, an individual's commitment to their place of work. He says there are two types of commitment.

- ◪ External commitment, or contractual compliance. This is the sort of commitment that employees display under the command-and-control type of structure, when they have little control over their own destiny and little idea of how to change things.
- ◪ Internal commitment is something that occurs when employees are committed to a particular project or person for their own individual reasons. Internal commitment, said Argyris, is closely allied with empowerment.

The problem with many corporate programmes designed to encourage empowerment is that they create more external than internal commitment. One reason, says Argyris, is that the programmes are riddled with contradictions and send out mixed messages, such as "do your own thing – the way we tell you". The result is that employees feel little responsibility for the programme, and people throughout the organisation feel less empowered.

Argyris suggests that companies should recognise that empowerment has its limits. It should not be a goal in itself; it is only a means to the ultimate goal of superior performance. Organisations should then set out to establish working conditions that encourage their employees' internal commitment, clearly recognising how this differs from the external variety.

Recommended reading

Argyris, C., "Empowerment: The Emperor's New Clothes", *Harvard Business Review*, May-June 1998

Kanter, R.M., "Power Failures in Management Circuits", *Harvard Business Review*, July-August 1979

Kanter, R.M., *When Giants Learn to Dance*, Simon & Schuster, 1989

Malone, T.W., "Is 'Empowerment' Just a Fad?", *Sloan Management Review*, Winter 1997

Enterprise resource planning

Enterprise resource planning (ERP) is the setting up of electronic information systems throughout an organisation in such a way that they bring together disparate parts that may rarely in the past have had access to information about each other. ERP software, designed to implement this, acts as a sort of central nervous system for the corporation. It gathers information about the state and activity of different parts of the body corporate and conveys this information to parts elsewhere that can make fruitful use of it. The information is updated in real time by the users and is accessible to all those on the network at all times.

Just as the central nervous system's capacity can at times seem to transcend the sum of the capacity of its individual parts (a phenomenon that we call consciousness), so too can that of ERP systems. They (as it were) make the corporation self-aware. In particular, ERP systems link together information about finance, human resources, production and distribution. They embrace stock-control systems, customer databases, order-tracking systems, accounts payable, and so on. They also interface when and where necessary with suppliers and customers.

The interlinking of ERP systems can be extraordinarily complex, and firms usually start with a pilot project before implementing a group-wide system.

A brief history

The history of ERP is the history of SAP, a German software company that in the 1990s established an extraordinary dominance of the ERP market. SAP (System Analyse und Programmentwicklung) was set up by three engineers in Mannheim in 1972. Their aim was to help companies link their different business processes by correlating information from various functions and using it to run the whole business more smoothly.

SAP's software was designed to be modular so that a company's systems could be rapidly adapted to take account of growth and change. It was so successful in recognising and meeting business's IT needs that by the late 1990s SAP's share of the market for ERP systems was greater than that of its five nearest rivals combined. Its systems were reckoned to be running in at least half of the world's 500 largest companies.

Its extraordinarily rapid growth (an annual average rate of growth of sales of over 40%) was backed by a marketing strategy that encouraged management consultants to implement SAP systems within client firms. Many consultants set up specialist SAP departments for the purpose. Without this support in implementation, there would have been a crippling bottleneck in the growth of SAP's sales.

The ERP systems market itself grew rapidly as firms saw the benefits to be gained from consolidating information about their geographically and functionally dispersed bits and pieces. ERP systems enabled them to have a view of their organisation as a whole that they had never previously experienced. It was like seeing the early colour photographs of earth taken from outer space.

Initially, such systems were most popular with large multinationals, which had a number of characteristics that made them particularly receptive.

- They had advanced IT infrastructures on which they could run the systems.
- They were keen to standardise their diverse range of business processes.
- They had the necessary staff to manage the systems once they were up and running.

As this big-company market became saturated, however, ERP systems providers began to look at how they might moderate their products to suit smaller organisations.

Recommended reading

Shtub, A., *Enterprise Resource Planning: the Dynamics of Operations Management*, Kluwer Academic Publishers, 1999

Welti, N., *Successful SAP Implementation: Practical Management of ERP Projects*, Addison-Wesley, 1999

Entrepreneurship

Jean-Baptiste Say, a French economist who first coined the word entrepreneur in about 1800, said: "The entrepreneur shifts economic resources out of an area of lower and into an area of higher productivity and greater yield." One dictionary says an entrepreneur is "one who undertakes an enterprise, especially a contractor acting as the intermediary between capital and labour".

Entrepreneurship is the special collection of skills possessed by an entrepreneur. They include a propensity to take risks over and above the normal, and a desire to create wealth. Entrepreneurs are people who find ways round business difficulties; they persevere with a business plan at times when others run for the shelter of full-time employment. This may be either because they have a great vision (see page 238), or because they are determined to feature on the world's lists of richest people. It may also be because they are recklessly stubborn, or because they are determined to show that they are not the worthless scoundrels that their parents always said they were.

Many conservative governments have tried to create a positive atmosphere for entrepreneurs in order to encourage their capitalist endeavour and wealth creation. Socialist governments, however, have generally regarded entrepreneurs as opportunists, people who would sell their grandmothers if they could be floated on a stockmarket. They are, such governments maintain, people who need to be controlled. Some academics have encouraged such a view. Abraham Zaleznik, a Harvard Business School professor, once said, "I think if we want to understand the entrepreneur, we should look at the juvenile delinquent".

A brief history

Until recently, there was a general feeling that entrepreneurs were born not made. The skills they required were, it was thought, either learned at the dinner table when young, or they were instinctive, a "seat of the pants" thing. *The Economist* wrote, "Entrepreneurs – the most successful, though not the only, practitioners of innovation [see page 116] – rarely stop to examine how they do it."

The main constraint on entrepreneurs has always been considered to be finance. The old picture was of the entrepreneur, brimming with bright ideas, beating a path to the closed doors of one bank after another.

In recent years, however, a whole industry has grown up, the venture-capital industry, to meet the financial needs of entrepreneurs and to share in the fruits of their endeavour; that is, to take equity in their ventures.

For most entrepreneurs, the pot of gold at the end of the rainbow usually lies in obtaining a listing on a quoted stock exchange and then selling shares through a public offering. A number of small exchanges have been set up in developed economies to encourage small entrepreneurial firms to follow precisely this route. The expense of obtaining a quotation on one of the traditional stock exchanges (such as New York or London) has been prohibitively high for most entrepreneurial companies. However, entrepreneurs generally run small businesses because this is the only way that they can keep complete control of the operation. They often have great internal difficulty in growing into large, established businesses.

Some management writers have tried to take the idea of entrepreneurship into big organisations, encouraging full-time employees (on monthly salaries and the promise of a pension) to think like entrepreneurs. This idea has been dubbed "intrapreneurship".

Recommended reading

Drucker, P., *Innovation and Entrepreneurship: Practice and Principles*, Harper & Row, 1985

Jennings, R., Cox, C. and Cooper, C., *Business Elites: the Psychology of Entrepreneurs and Intrapreneurs*, Van Nostrand Reinhold, 1994

Venture Capital, an International Journal of Entrepreneurial Finance, www.taylorandfrancis.com

Ethical business

"Business is business, and Moses is Moses", runs an old Jewish saying; that is, do not mix business with morals, family, religion or any of the other things with which Moses is associated. Nevertheless, there was increasing pressure on companies throughout the 20th century (particularly towards the end of it) to mix business and Moses; that is, to take ethical considerations more seriously into account in their everyday dealings.

The big question – "What does it mean for a business to be ethical?" – had a significant subtext – "Is it to possible to be an ethical business at the same time as trying to maximise profit?".

Many international conventions have been held to consider these issues, and many papers with titles like "A framework for assessing the relationship between trade liberalisation and biodiversity conservation" have been published. Nevertheless, most firms remain unclear as to what they should do to be deemed to be ethical.

Three main strands to the ethical issue seem to have emerged.

Environmental
This has stretched way beyond the simple demand that companies stop belching smoke out of factory chimneys to a demand that they control their appetite for natural resources, for bits of Brazilian rain forest, for example, or for the skins of rare animals. The issue is rarely clear cut, however. Where should the lines be drawn? Is it really unethical to sell fur coats? Humans have always worn animal skins, and nobody gets upset about sheepskins. So is it only the selling of endangered species that is unethical? The mink is not endangered; far from it. Yet protesters released farmed minks into the British countryside in what seemed more like a protest against the wealth that can afford to buy fur than against the treatment of the minks themselves. Nevertheless, suppliers frightened by the venom of the anti-fur lobby have felt compelled to boast: "Make no mistake; all our furs are fake."

Exploitation
The second strand is the exploitation of workers, especially of women in the developed world and of children in the developing world. There is a feeling that the process of globalisation (see page 106), as it has increased

the power of multinationals, has weakened the influence of trade unions and other workers' organisations. But if western companies did not buy the output of under-age workers in, say, the Indian subcontinent, would they not be depriving that continent of much-needed export earnings?

Some see the export of ethical standards on working conditions as a kind of cultural imperialism designed to hold back developing countries by preventing them from passing through a natural (if, for the West, Dickensian) phase of industrial development. Again the issue focuses on what should the standards be, how should they be measured, and once they have been measured how should their observance be enforced.

Corruption
The third strand focuses on corruption, in particular the issue of what constitutes a bribe (when does over-generous corporate hospitality become corruption?) and what protections should be given to whistle-blowers (employees or other insiders who report misdeeds occurring within corporations).

Once again there is a strong cultural element. What constitutes bribery in western countries is not considered as such in places like the Middle East. Many companies give their employees guidelines about receiving hospitality. British Gas (BG) is not atypical:

> *While it is recognised that limited corporate hospitality is given and received as part of building normal business relationships, staff should avoid accepting hospitality or gifts which might appear to place them under an obligation.*
>
> *Bribery of any form is unacceptable. No undeclared offers or payments will be accepted or solicited by BG staff, or made by BG staff to third parties, and staff are required to avoid any contacts that might lead to, or suggest, a conflict of interest between their personal activities and the business of the Company.*

A brief history

In 1987 Adrian Cadbury, head of the famous chocolate firm, wrote in the *Harvard Business Review*:

> *The possibility that ethical and commercial considerations will conflict has always faced those who run companies. It*

> *is not a new problem. The difference now is that a more widespread and critical interest is being taken in our decisions and in the ethical judgements which lie behind them.*

Many large companies now state publicly their ethical principles. John Harvey-Jones, a former chairman of the UK chemicals group ICI, once said: "It horrifies me that ethics is only an optional extra at the Harvard Business School". Nobody would have thought to say that in the 1960s.

Many businesses have come to realise that a cost-benefit analysis (see page 43) of the decision to become an ethical business can be strongly positive. There are large premiums to be gained from the growing number of consumers who are prepared to pay in order to feel good about the products that they buy. "Being good", said Anita Roddick, founder of an "ethical" cosmetics firm, The Body Shop, "is good business". (See also Mission statement, page 154.)

In the United States the Better Business Bureau argues that unethical business is bad for business as a whole, not just for individual firms: "Unethical business practices create ill-will among customers and the community, not only toward a particular business firm, but toward business as a whole."

Recommended reading

Carroll, S.J. and Gannon, M.J., *Ethical Dimensions of International Management, Sage Series in Business Ethics*, Sage, 1997

Davies, P., *Current Issues in Business Ethics*, Routledge, 1997

Donaldson, T. and Gini, A. (eds), *Case Studies in Business Ethics*, Prentice-Hall, 1993

Reinhardt, Forest (sic) L., "Bringing the Environment down to Earth", *Harvard Business Review*, July-August 1999

Roddick, A., *Body and Soul*, Ebury Press, 1991

Excellence

Following the publication in 1982 of the best-selling management book of all time – *In Search of Excellence*, written by two consultants, Tom Peters and Robert Waterman – a movement grew up behind the main idea in the book, the idea of excellence. The authors claimed to have found eight attributes that characterised what they defined as excellent companies in the United States (the subtext read "try them and you can be excellent too"). These were as follows.

1 **A bias for action.** In many of these companies, claimed the authors, the standard operating procedure is "Do it, fix it, try it".

2 **Close to the customer.** Excellent companies "learn from the people they serve".

3 **Autonomy and entrepreneurship.** The authors quote one description of 3M, a leading role model: it is "so intent on innovation that its essential atmosphere seems not like that of a large corporation, but rather a loose network of laboratories and cubbyholes populated by feverish inventors and dauntless entrepreneurs who let their imaginations fly in all directions".

4 **Productivity through people.** Excellent companies have a deep-seated respect for the rank and file and do not regard "capital investment as the fundamental source of efficiency improvement".

5 **Hands-on, value driven.** In excellent companies the top managers believe in management by walking about (MBWA, see page 144).

6 **Stick to the knitting.** "The odds for excellent performance seem strongly to favour those companies that stay reasonably close to businesses they know."

7 **Simple form, lean staff.** Simple form means having no matrix management (see page 150), and an organisation in which "it is not uncommon to find a corporate [headquarters] staff of fewer than 100 people running multibillion dollar enterprises".

8 **Simultaneous loose-tight properties.** "Excellent companies are both centralised and decentralised."

The last was perhaps the most difficult of all the attributes to understand and put into effect. As the authors wrote: "Most of these eight attributes are not startling. Some, if not most, are motherhoods."

A brief history

In Search of Excellence sold many million copies, far more than any other management book in the 20th century. By being eminently readable – it tells rollicking good stories about interesting companies – it brought the ideas of business and management to a much wider audience than had ever gained access to them before. It could only do this, of course, with the help of considerable simplification. This simplification, although being the cause of its success, has been criticised as a weakness. Peter Drucker, a leading management academic, said that the book "makes managing sound so incredibly easy. All you have to do is put that book under your pillow, and it'll get done".

Peters and Waterman based their ideas largely on experience they had gained from working with American companies when they were employed as management consultants by McKinsey in the late 1970s and early 1980s. There they had been in contact with a fellow consultant, Richard Pascale, who had taken McKinsey's idea of the Seven Ss (see page 198) and used its framework to explain the growing superiority (at the time) of Japanese industry and management methods (expounded in his book *The Art of Japanese Management*).

American industry was demoralised by its alleged inability to compete with this new industrial giant in the east, and Peters and Waterman gave its morale just the boost it needed. Look, they said, all is not gloom and doom. We have found a large number of companies within the United States that are excellent at all seven of the Ss, the elements that together make for corporate success.

The fact that many of Peters and Waterman's so-called excellent companies subsequently stumbled into something less than excellence (Peters declared loudly in a later book that "there are no excellent companies") did not diminish the popularity of the two men's message. Indeed, almost from the moment that the book was published, corporate America began to rise to new heights of productivity and growth that no other country was to match in the 20th century.

Kathryn Harrigan, a business school professor, attributed some of the book's success to the fact that "Americans are into cults, particularly the cult of the personality. They are all looking for the recipe of success, and Tom Peters made the best job of that. People knew exactly where to place him".

Peters became the leader of a new generation of management experts who took their wisdom off the bookshelf and into the classroom. Energetic, lively and entertaining, he wowed crowds of executives in conference halls from Hamburg to Hong Kong, the leader of a regular (and highly influential) migration of American gurus spreading the gospel of American management excellence to all the corners of the earth.

Robert Waterman was the direct opposite of Peters. Shy and introspective, he stayed on at McKinsey long after Peters had left. He eventually set up his own consultancy in San Francisco.

Recommended reading

Peters, T. and Waterman, R., *In Search of Excellence*, Harper and Row, 1982

Peters, T. and Austin, N., *A Passion for Excellence*, Collins, 1985

Peters, T., *Thriving on Chaos*, Alfred A. Knopf, 1987

Waterman, R., *The Renewal Factor*, Bantam, 1987

The experience curve

The experience curve is an idea that was developed by the Boston Consulting Group (BCG) in the mid-1960s. Working with a leading manufacturer of semiconductors, the consultants noticed that the company's unit cost of manufacturing fell by about 25% for each doubling of the volume that it produced. This relationship it called the experience curve: the more experience a firm has in producing a particular product, the lower are its costs. Bruce Henderson, the founder of BCG, put it as follows:

> Costs characteristically decline by 20–30% in real terms each time accumulated experience doubles. This means that when inflation is factored out, costs should always decline. The decline is fast if growth is fast and slow if growth is slow.

There is no fundamental economic law that can predict the existence of the experience curve, even though the curve has been shown to apply to all industries across the board. Its truth has been proven inductively, not deductively.

By itself, the curve is not particularly earth shattering. Even when BCG first expounded the relationship, it had been known since the second world war that it applied to direct labour costs. Less labour was needed for a given output depending on the experience of that labour. In aircraft production, for instance, labour input decreased by some 10–15% for every doubling of that labour's experience.

The strategic implications of the experience curve came closer to shattering earth. For if costs fell (fairly predictably) with experience, and if experience was closely related to market share (as it seemed it must be), then the competitor with the biggest market share was going to have a big cost advantage over its rivals. QED: being market leader is a valuable asset that a firm relinquishes at its peril.

This was the logic underpinning the idea of the growth share matrix (see page 109). It justified allocating financial resources to those businesses (out of a firm's portfolio of businesses) that were (or were going to be) market leaders in their particular sectors. To do this, of course, implied starvation for those businesses that were not and never would be.

A brief history

Over time, managers came to see the experience curve as being too imprecise to help them much with specific business plans. Once the strategic implications of the general principle had been taken on board, there seemed little point in pursuing it any further.

Inconveniently, different products had curves of a different slope and different sources of cost reduction. They did not, for instance, all have the same downward gradient as the semiconductor industry. A study by the Rand Corporation found that "a doubling in the number of [nuclear] reactors [built by an architect-engineer] results in a 5% reduction in both construction time and capital cost."

Part of the explanation for this discrepancy was that different products provided different opportunities to gain experience. Large products (such as nuclear reactors) are inherently bound to be produced in smaller volumes than small products (such as semiconductors). It is not easy for a firm to double the volume of production of something that it takes over five years to build, and where the total market may never be more than a few hundred units.

In theory, the experience curve should make it difficult for new entrants to challenge firms with a substantial market share. In practice, new firms enter old industries all the time, and before long many of them become major players in their markets. This is often because they have found ways of bypassing what might seem like the remorseless inevitability of the curve and its slope. For example, experience can be gained not only first-hand – by actually doing the production and finding out for yourself – but also second-hand, by reading about it and by being trained by people who do have experience. Furthermore, firms can leapfrog over the experience curve by means of innovation and invention. All the experience in the world in making black and white televisions is worthless if everyone wants to buy colour sets.

Recommended reading

De Bono, E., *Practical Thinking*, Penguin, 1971

Ghemawat, P., "Building Strategy on the Experience Curve", *Harvard Business Review*, March-April 1985

Henderson, B.D., *The Logic of Business Strategy*, Ballinger Publishing, 1984

Sallenare, J.P., "The Uses and Abuses of Experience Curves", *Long Range Planning*, Vol. 18, No. 1, 1985

Stern, C.W. and Stalk, G. Jr (eds), *Perspectives on Strategy from BCG*, John Wiley, 1998

Family firms

Family firms have become big business. They have their own magazine, *Family Business*, their own specialist community of consultants, and their own academic institutions – for example, the Loyola University Chicago Family Business Center.

The Institute for Family Enterprise at Bryant College in Rhode Island defines a family firm as:

> *An enterprise that has been in the control of a single family since inception. It can be either private or public, so long as family members have an input in the operation and future of the business.*

Although the family firm itself cannot fairly be described as a management idea, it does embody a number of distinctive features around which has been spun a specific theory about corporate behaviour. One of the distinctive features of the family firm, said an economist, Alfred Marshall, is that "the master's eye is everywhere". This inevitably brings the successful family firm into a conflict between the master's need for control and the firm's need for growth.

Other distinctive features of family businesses include the following.

Their age
Contrary to the general impression, the average life span of a family firm is less than that of a public company. Although it is said that it takes one generation to make it, one to enjoy it and one to lose it, few family businesses continue into the third generation. The idea that they live much longer stems from the fact that a number of them have continued in business for a remarkable length of time. Japan's Hoshi Hotel, for example, claims to have been run as a family firm since 718AD. Europe's longest running family businesses come from Italy, where Barovier & Toso, a Venetian glassmaker, was established in 1295 and the Beretta family has been making guns since 1526.

The most prolific creator of family firms, the United States, cannot boast such longevity. The Institute for Family Enterprise says that the oldest family firm in the United States is Tuttle Market Gardens, founded in 1636. The *Wall Street Journal*'s candidate for "oldest family business" in the United States is a company called Zildjian Cymbal. It did not qualify for the institute's award, however, because it has spent most of its life in another country. It was founded in Istanbul in 1623 and only relocated to Norwell, Massachusetts, in 1929.

A different attitude to growth

Many economists believe that family firms, when they reach a certain size, restrain growth. As very small businesses they are ebullient promoters of it, but at a certain stage a sort of sclerosis sets in. Well-established family firms, for example, often resist mergers and acquisitions for fear of losing control to outsiders, and (maybe) of having the family's name disappear from over the front door of the company's headquarters.

It is no coincidence that the massive shift that has taken place during the 20th century, from the predominance of the family firm to the predominance of the public corporation, has been paralleled by a shift from a corporate culture in which growth was one of a number of long-term goals to a culture in which it was the predominant goal by far.

A survey of American family businesses in 1995 found that the firms which recorded high growth in turnover were more likely to have:

◾ international sales;
◾ a strategic plan; and
◾ more than three board meetings a year.

Problems with succession

These generally fall into two categories.

The first is dealing with members of the family themselves. Who is to be groomed to take over at the helm? After two or three generations there can be a number of competing cousins, who, if they are not to be groomed for the top, want out. This can create all sorts of problems that a public company does not have to face. To resolve them a new breed of dispute resolution specialists has grown up, most of whom have legal or counselling qualifications.

The second problem is how to hold on to good non-family employees who know that the very top seats are denied to them.

A brief history

Etna M. Kelley, a business historian, once noted that, "for reasons unknown, funeral homes and seed companies – symbolic of death and life – seem to last a long time". Both industries have always been strongly represented among the longest-lasting family firms. However, there have been plenty of family firms that were nothing like the "Mom-and-Pop" funeral parlour. In the 1890s a thread manufacturer, J&P Coats, effectively controlled the world's textiles industry at a time when its board was in the hands of a very few members of the Coats family. When the Ford Motor Company dominated the American automobile industry, at the end of the first world war, it was wholly owned by two men, Henry Ford and his son, Edsel.

Over the years, the number of large corporations that could be defined as family firms has dwindled in all major economies. In the UK most of the decline came in the second half of the 20th century. In 1930, 70% of the 200 largest companies in the UK still had members of their founding families on the board. By the end of the second world war that figure had fallen to 60%. By the 1970s the number of really large UK companies that could be called family firms had dwindled to a few, such as McAlpine (in construction), Ferranti (in electronics) and the Vesteys' group (in meat and foods).

Although family connections remain in a few large companies today, in retailers like Wal-Mart and Sainsbury's and in car companies like Ford and Fiat, none of these giants can be said in any sense to be run like a family firm. (See also Succession planning, page 213.)

Recommended reading

Donnelly, R.G., "The Family Business", Harvard Business Review, July-August 1964

Gersick, K.E., Davis, J.A., McCollom Hampton, M. and Lansberg, I., Generation to Generation: Life Cycles of the Family Business, Harvard Business School Press, 1997

Levinson, H., "Conflicts that Plague the Family Business", Harvard Business Review, January-February, 1971

Miller, W.D., "Siblings and Succession in the Family Business", Harvard Business Review, January-February, 1998

Neubauer, F. and Lank, A., The Family Business, Macmillan, 1998

The Family Business Review, Family Firm Institute, Brookline, MA, United States

Franchising

Franchising is a way for firms to increase their turnover without increasing their assets. One of the best known franchises is the McDonald's chain of hamburger restaurants. Approximately 80% of McDonald's restaurant businesses around the world are owned and operated by franchisees. However, almost every type of business has been franchised, from Big Apple Bagels to DreamMaker Baths & Kitchens.

Franchising involves two parties, the franchiser and the franchisee. The franchiser owns a trademark or brand which he (or she) agrees to allow the franchisee to use for a fee (often an original purchase price plus a percentage of sales). The franchiser provides the franchisee with assistance (financial, choice of site, and so on) in setting up their operation, and then maintains continuing control over various aspects of the franchisee's business; for example, via the supply of products, discussion of marketing plans and/or centralised staff training.

The franchisee buys into a proven business plan and considerable expertise. Other advantages of franchising to the franchisee include cost savings from the bulk buying capacity of a large operation, and the marketing benefits of central advertising and promotion of the business.

Many franchisees sign a franchise agreement believing it to be less risky than setting up a business on their own. Things can go badly wrong, however, even with well-known and well-established franchise operations. Some franchisers have antagonised their franchisees by selling new franchises for sites close to existing operations. Many contracts now stipulate that franchises cannot be sold less than a certain distance apart.

Franchising has been subject to some smart practices, and in many American states there is now legislation controlling the sale of franchises. This is similar to legislation controlling the sale of securities, often requiring the franchiser to disclose regular financial and other details to the state authorities.

McDonald's, the doyen of franchisers, says that its system is successful because it is "built on the premise that the corporation should only make money from its franchisees' food sales, which avoids the potential conflicts of interest that exist in so many franchising operations [where fees are not tied so closely to sales]. All our franchisees are independent, full-time franchisees rather than conglomerates or passive investors".

McDonald's also says that it is "committed to franchising as our predominant way of doing business".

A brief history

Franchising became popular in a rash of enthusiasm for decentralised organisational structures at the end of the 20th century. However, elements from the idea of franchising have been used for centuries. An article in the McKinsey Quarterly (No. 1, 1998) says:

> The 18th-century North West Company featured decentralised decision making, a franchise-like structure, and strong incentive systems, features that enabled it to overtake the entrenched Hudson's Bay Company despite its overwhelming structural advantages.

In the 1980s Benetton gained wide publicity for its use of franchising to enable it to concentrate on a few core competencies (see page 40). It franchised the retailing of its garments and outsourced (see page 163) their manufacture to small workshops around northern Italy.

Growth in franchising was fast. By 1999 the International Franchise Association reckoned that:

> More than 540,000 franchise businesses dot the American landscape, generating more than $800 billion in sales. With a new franchise business opening somewhere in the US every 6.5 minutes each business day, franchising is indeed the success story of the 1990s.

It has been particularly popular in the fast-food sector – not just hamburger joints but also coffee shops, the Kentucky Fried Chicken (now KFC) chain and more upmarket eateries. The Avis car-rental business is a franchise operation as are several hotel chains, such as Marriott and Oriental.

Franchises can bring great wealth to both parties; but they can also be a disaster for both parties. A restaurant franchise in the UK called Pierre Victoire was started in 1987 by Pierre Levicky, a Frenchman living in Edinburgh. By 1996 there were over 100 Pierre Victoire outlets in the UK and Levicky was planning to float his business on the London stockmarket with a valuation of £14m. But a number of problems (not least a lack of control over the franchise quality) led to the receivers being called into the company in 1998. Some of the franchisees took over the business; others had to abandon their restaurants' name. Levicky ended up as a chef in one of his former franchisee's restaurants.

Recommended reading

Bradach, J.L., *Franchise Organizations*, Harvard Business School Press, 1998

Konigsberg, A., *International Franchising*, Sweet & Maxwell, 1997

Shook, C., Shook, R.L. and Cherkasky, W.B., *Franchising: The Business Strategy That Changed the World*, Prentice-Hall, 1993

Game theory

The idea of business as a game, in the sense that a move by one player sparks off moves by others, runs through much strategic thinking. It is borrowed from a branch of economics (game theory) in which no economic agent (individual or corporate) is an island, living and acting independently of everybody else.

In industry sectors where firms compete fiercely for market share and customer loyalty, this stylised progression of moves closely parallels actual behaviour. Few firms nowadays think about strategy without adding a bit of game theory to their thinking. For von Neumann and Morgenstern, the two economists who developed the idea of game theory, strategy was "a complete plan: a plan which specifies what choices [the player] will make in every possible situation".

Seeing business life as a never-ending series of games, each of which has a winner and a loser, can be a handicap. In business negotiations, for example, with external suppliers or customers, or with trade unions or colleagues, it can hinder a satisfactory conclusion if the participants see it only in terms of a victory or a loss. Because that way someone has to walk away feeling bad about the outcome. In some non-western cultures the aim is different. The negotiation process is steered towards a win-win outcome, one with which both parties can be reasonably content.

Business is sometimes said most closely to resemble the game of chess. Several successful businessmen have been skilled chess players, such as Robert Holmes à Court, an Australian tycoon. But chess is a game for only two players, and business is rarely a duopoly. If anything, it is a game involving many players, each of which is playing all the others.

A brief history

The language of business is scattered with references to games. Regulators try to ensure that companies operate on a "level playing field", and competition is, according to at least one dictionary, "a series of games". Business games that have enjoyed (sometimes brief) popularity include the following.

The end game

This is a strategy that a company evolves for a product that seems to be on its last legs. Should the company bleed the product for all it is worth before it dies? Or should it introduce an aggressive pricing policy aimed at forcing its competitors out of business and allowing it to continue in a much reduced niche market? In her book *Managing Maturing Businesses*, a Harvard professor, Kathryn Harrigan, argues that end games can be highly profitable. She writes: "The last surviving player makes money serving the last bit of demand, when the competitors drop away."

The croquet game
In *The Change Masters*, Rosabeth Moss Kanter wrote:

> *I think the game that best describes most businesses today is the croquet game in Alice in Wonderland. In that game nothing remains stable for very long. Everything is changing around the players. Alice goes to hit a ball, but her mallet is a flamingo. Just as she's about to hit the ball, the flamingo lifts its head and looks in another direction. That's just like technology and the tools that we use.*

The win-win game
This is a game where both parties end up as winners, for example, a merger between two companies where synergy (see page 218) genuinely allows them to become more than the sum of their parts.

The new product development game
This was the title of a popular article in the January-February 1986 issue of the *Harvard Business Review*.

The zero sum game
This is shorthand for the idea that every game, be it in business or on the sports field, has a winner and a loser. The winner's win plus the loser's loss equal zero. In such a game there is no incentive to co-operate with opponents because every inch given to them is an inch lost. The idea of the zero sum game is modified by the introduction of the possibility of change in the nature of the game while it is being played. Hence, for instance, companies that are fighting for market share are playing a zero sum game if they see that market as fixed. But if the market is continually expanding (or if the companies redefine it so that it is), then the players are playing a game in which they can have a smaller share of a bigger cake and still see their businesses grow.

There are of course all kinds of other games that people play in business to exert power and influence in an organisation or to outwit and stay ahead of competitors.

Recommended reading

Berne, E., *Games People Play*, André Deutsch, 1964

Friedman, S.D., Christensen, P. and DeGroot, J., "Work and Life: the End of the Zero Sum Game", *Harvard Business Review*, November-December 1998

Harrigan, K., *Managing Maturing Businesses*, Lexington Books, 1988

McDonald, J., *Strategy in Poker, Business and War*, W.W. Norton, 1950

Shubik, M., *Games for Society, Business and War: Towards a Theory of Gaming*, Elsevier, 1975

Sun Tzu, *The Art of War*, 500 BC (OUP, 1963)

Von Neumann, J. and Morgenstern, O., *Theory of Games and Economic Behaviour*, Princeton University Press, 1944

The glass ceiling

The glass ceiling is an invisible, artificial barrier that prevents qualified individuals (particularly women) from advancing beyond a certain point within their employing organisation. The barrier's existence can be deduced from the fact that there is a stark difference between the proportion of women (and of minority groups) who graduate from the leading universities and business schools, and the proportion of women (and of minorities) who reach the higher echelons of corporate management. In the late 1980s, for example, only 500 of the top 6,700 managers at IBM and only 26 of the top 880 executives at AT&T were women.

A secondary issue is that of women's pay. There is evidence that even when women do reach the highest levels of corporate management, they do not receive the same pay as men for the same job; a figure of 70% is often quoted. A survey in 1992 showed women executives in the United States earning an average of $187,000 while male executives were earning an average of $289,000. American census data reported that the ratio of female to male earnings in management jobs ranged from a low of 50% in the banking industry to a high of 85% for human services managers.

A number of reasons have been put forward to explain the glass ceiling.

The time factor
One theory says that the cohorts of first-class female graduates have not yet had time to work through the pipeline and reach the top of the corporate hierarchy. Qualifications for a senior management post usually include a graduate degree and 25 years of continuous work experience. In 1970, when today's senior managers were graduating, fewer than 5% of law and MBA degrees were being awarded to women. Nowadays, women gain about 43% of all law degrees in the United States and 35% of MBAS.

So the number of female corporate executives can be expected to rise, as has been happening for some years. In 1972 in the United States, for instance, women accounted for only 17.6% of managerial posts; by 1983 the figure had risen to 32.4%. There has, however, been no comparable progress at the top of the corporate ladder.

Motherhood
Sometimes the blame for the glass ceiling is laid at the door of motherhood. Women are distracted from their career path by the need to

stay at home and rear children. Even if they return to work immediately, they fall behind their male colleagues on the career ladder. With babies to care for, they are unable to undertake the tasks that are often required to reach the top; for example, taking extended trips abroad, spending long evenings "entertaining" clients, and changing plans at short notice. Few companies attempt to eliminate this disadvantage, with the result that women generally stay in corporate functions (such as human resources or communications) that do not require them to perform these tasks. They then become narrowly specialised and cannot gain the broad-based experience that is usually demanded for the most senior posts.

Male stereotypes

Others maintain that the glass ceiling has more to do with male stereotypes of women than with anything else. In many companies these stereotypes have become institutionalised. The standards for advancement, for instance, are set by white male graduates, and women who want to progress are judged by these standards.

We all think we should be replaced by someone who is exactly like us. After all we were perfect for the job, weren't we? Most senior managers' succession planning (see page 213) is guided by this principle. In her 1977 book *Men and Women of the Corporation*, Rosabeth Moss Kanter suggested that because managerial women are so often a token female in their work environment they stand out from the rest. This makes them (and their failures) much more visible, and exaggerates the differences between them and the dominant male culture.

A brief history

The expression seems to have been used first by A.M. Morrison and others in a 1987 article entitled "Breaking the Glass Ceiling: Can Women reach the top of America's Largest Corporations?". The following year a book by Marilyn Davidson and Gary Cooper was published entitled *Shattering the Glass Ceiling*.

By 1991 the American government had created something called The Glass Ceiling Commission. This was a 21-member body appointed by the president and Congress and chaired by the labour secretary. As part of the Civil Rights Act, the commission worked to identify so-called glass ceiling barriers and to encourage practices and policies that promote opportunities for the advancement of women into positions of responsibility in private-sector employment. The commission focused on barriers and opportunities in three areas:

- the filling of management and decision-making positions;
- skills-enhancing activities; and
- compensation and reward systems.

The Glass Ceiling Commission "completed its mandate" in 1996 and was disbanded.

Recommended reading

Davidson, M. and Cooper, G., *Shattering the Glass Ceiling*, PCP, 1988

Kanter, R.M., *Men and Women of the Corporation*, Basic Books, 1977

Morrison, A.M. and Von Glinow, M.A., "Women and Minorities in Management", *American Psychologist*, 1990

Tavris, C., *The Mismeasure of Women*, Simon and Schuster, 1992

"Women and Work", *The Economist*, 18th July 1998

http://www.ilr.cornell.edu – copies of the Glass Ceiling Commission's fact-finding report, *Good for Business: Making Full Use of the Nation's Human Capital*, and the recommendations report, *A Solid Investment: Making Full Use of the Nation's Human Capital*

Globalisation

Globalisation is the successful attempt by companies to sell the same product or service simultaneously in many different markets around the world. The spread of globalisation over the past few decades has been so wide that nobody is surprised to see Coca-Cola in rural Vietnam, Shell petrol stations in eastern Turkey or Nike shoes in Nigeria. Markets and tastes everywhere have converged at a rapid rate.

Globalisation has taken place in a number of ways. Some companies have chosen to export from a few domestic production facilities, largely to enable them to reap the huge economies of scale (see page 76) that can come from feeding the markets of the world from a small number of factories. Some companies, such as McDonald's, Pizza Hut and Hertz Rent-a-Car, have gone global by setting up franchise (see page 97) operations in foreign markets. Yet other companies have chosen to set up multinational manufacturing facilities with plants in a number of different countries.

The main debate about globalisation has focused not on whether it is happening, but on the best way to go about it. The principal questions have been: should companies try to integrate themselves closely into the local markets in which they sell; or should they stand apart and ship out uniform products from centralised production facilities?

Many of the companies with the most global products are remarkably national. Gillette sells razor blades everywhere, but it manufactures them in only a few places and tightly controls the process from the United States. Citibank has branched out into all the major cities of the world, but wherever it goes it remains American, an outsider. American Express even bears its nationality in its name. Some companies have changed from one strategy to another. Robert Goizueta, when chief executive of Coca-Cola, said: "We used to be an American company with a large international business. Now we're a large international company with a sizeable American business."

Some Japanese corporations have gone through a similar change. In their early days they shipped vast quantities of electronics goods and motor cars from tightly controlled production facilities inside Japan. However, they gradually changed their strategy in the 1980s as Japan came under international pressure to reduce its huge trade surplus and as the companies began to see other benefits from opening factories inside the main markets that they served.

In this they were influenced by the only internationally known Japanese management expert, Kenichi Ohmae. In two books, *Triad Power* and *The Borderless World*, he expounded the view that companies which did not have a full presence in the world's three main trading blocs (Europe, the United States and the Pacific Rim) were dangerously vulnerable to competition from those that did. "The word 'overseas' has no place in Honda's vocabulary," he wrote, "because it sees itself as equidistant from all its key customers." This Japanese view was most famously expressed in the Sony slogan devised by its founder, Akio Morita: "Global localisation".

In the United States, the idea of global localisation has not had such a warm reception (although Coca-Cola is an obvious exception). In an article on the globalisation of markets in the *Harvard Business Review* of May-June 1983, Theodore Levitt foresaw "the emergence of global markets for standardised consumer products on a previously unimagined scale of magnitude. Corporations geared to this new reality benefit from enormous economies of scale in production, distribution, marketing and management". This argued for the national producer distributing its products globally.

Bruce Kogut, a professor of management at Wharton School of Business, has argued (against Ohmae) that the national characteristics of multinational companies do not undermine their global competitiveness. As goods and people can move freely across borders, he says that companies are increasingly able to compete on a worldwide basis without straying far from their headquarters. The theory of competitive advantage (see page 35) says that companies generally specialise in whatever their country of operation does best. This specialisation, says Kogut, can actually strengthen national differences, not weaken them.

Some people saw a new sort of global organisation beginning to emerge towards the end of the 20th century, in which groups of specialists from different countries link together to produce final goods and services that customers demand. The glue that holds them together is information, not ownership, although they may be joined formally in a partnership or a temporary alliance.

A brief history

European companies are more accustomed to working in foreign markets than American or Japanese companies. The small size of most of their local markets has always forced them to look abroad at an early stage. One well-known European global company is Heineken, a Dutch brewery established more than 130 years ago, which sells beer in 170 different countries. The chairman, Karel Vuursteen, described the extent of the company's globalisation in an interview in 1998. It illustrates how national is the company's product and how global is its brand.

Heineken has a strict list of do's and don'ts. Vuursteen says:

> The don'ts are even more important than the do's. Our employees are not permitted to alter a single line on the label, lighten the packaging colours or adapt the shape of the bottle. Change any of this by one iota and you risk eroding the brand.
>
> In the same way we don't believe in adapting to local taste differences. The product must be the same everywhere. To ensure quality, every 14 days our breweries send samples to professional tasters in the Netherlands. We also buy back our beer from small shops as far away as Shanghai for testing purposes.

In marketing and advertising, on the other hand, Mr Vuursteen says:

> We don't believe you can communicate to all cultures in the same way. In the United States and Western Europe, beer is a normal part of life, it's thirst-quenching. In Australia and New Zealand, it's very macho. In many South-East Asian countries it's almost a "feminine" product – sophisticated. Thus, we give our local representatives a lot of freedom in sales and advertising.

Recommended reading

Doremus, P.N., Keller, W.W., Pauly, L.W. and Reich, S., *The Myth of the Global Corporation*, 1999 (paperback)

Hout, T., Porter, M. and Rudden, E., "How Global Companies Win Out", *Harvard Business Review*, September-October, 1982

Levitt, T., "The Globalisation of Markets", *Harvard Business Review*, May-June 1983

Ohmae, K., *Triad Power, The Coming Shape of Global Competition*, Free Press, 1985

Ohmae, K., *The Borderless World*, HarperBusiness, 1990

Growth share matrix

The growth share matrix is a framework developed by the Boston Consulting Group (BCG) in the 1960s to help companies think about the priority (and resources) that they should give to the different businesses in their portfolio. Commonly known as the Boston matrix, it puts these businesses individually into one of four categories, each with a memorable name. These names – cash cow, star, dog and question mark – helped the four categories to sink into the collective consciousness of managers all over the world. The two dimensions of the matrix are relative market share (or the ability to generate cash) and growth (or the need for cash).

- **Cash cows** are businesses that have a high market share (and are therefore generating lots of cash), but which have low growth prospects (and therefore a low need for cash). They are often in mature industries that are about to decline.
- **Stars** have high growth prospects and a high market share.
- **Question marks** have high growth prospects but a comparatively low market share (and have also been known as wild cats).
- **Dogs**, by deduction, are low on everything – growth prospects and market share.

The conclusions to be drawn from this analysis are that the surplus cash from a conglomerate's cash cows should be transferred to the stars and the question marks, and the dogs should be closed down or sold off. In the end, question marks have to reveal themselves as either dogs or stars, and cash cows become so drained of finance that they inevitably sooner or later turn into dogs.

The trouble with this colourful matrix is that classifying businesses in this way can be self-fulfilling. Knowing that you are working for a dog is not particularly motivating, whereas working for an acknowledged star usually is. Moreover, some companies misjudge when industries are mature. This leads them to decide that businesses are to be treated as cash cows when they are in fact stars. They may be in a business that is merely taking a break before surging forward again. One such industry was consumer electronics. Considered by many to be mature in the 1970s, it rebounded in the 1980s with the invention of the CD and the VCR. Not, however, before some companies had consigned their electronics businesses to the fate of the cash cow.

The growth share matrix has been blamed for causing companies to focus obsessively on market share. In a world where markets are increasingly fluid, this can cause them to lose their way. If Lego, for example, considers its market is mechanical toys, it misses out on the fact that it also competes with such companies as Nintendo for a share of young boys' minds.

The growth share matrix began a fashion among consultants for creating matrices. Now no self-respecting report or theory is complete without one or two. For that we have to thank BCG.

A brief history

Like a number of leading figures from the world of management theory, Bruce Doolin Henderson, the Australian founder of the Boston Consulting Group, was an engineer. One of his favourite quotations was a saying of Archimedes: "Give me a lever and a place to stand, and I'll move the world." Henderson used his own levers to great effect. He worked as a strategic planner for General Electric until joining the Arthur D. Little management consultancy, which he left in 1963 to set up the Boston Consulting Group. BCG rapidly established a reputation as the prime strategic consultancy. On his death in 1992, the *Financial Times* said of Henderson: "Few people have had as much impact on international business in the second half of the 20th century."

Henderson and the firm he created were pioneers in thinking about corporate strategy and competition. BCG was responsible for developing other enduring ideas besides the growth share matrix. These included the experience curve (the idea that unit costs decline as production increases because of the acquisition of experience; see page 92); the significance of being market leader; and time-based competition. Henderson liked to push ideas to the limit. He believed that "while most people understand first-order effects, few deal well with second- and third-order effects. Unfortunately, virtually everything interesting in business lies in fourth-order effects and beyond".

Recommended reading

Henderson, B., *Henderson on Corporate Strategy*, HarperBusiness, 1984
Stern, C. and Stalk, G. Jr (eds), *Perspectives on Strategy from the Boston Consulting Group*, John Wiley, 1998

The Hawthorne effect

The Hawthorne effect is named after what was undoubtedly the most famous experiment (or, more accurately, series of experiments) in industrial history. It marked a sea change in thinking about work and productivity. Previous studies, in particular the influential work of Frederick Taylor (see Scientific management, page 193), had focused on the individual and on the ways in which an individual's performance could be improved. Hawthorne set the individual in a social context. The experiment established conclusively that a worker's performance is influenced by their surroundings and by the people that they are working with. This principle has underscored much management thinking since.

A brief history

The experiments took place at Western Electric's factory at Hawthorne, a suburb of Chicago, in the late 1920s and early 1930s. They were conducted for the most part under the supervision of Elton Mayo, an Australian-born sociologist who eventually became professor of industrial research at Harvard.

The original purpose of the experiments was to study the effects of physical conditions on productivity. Two groups of workers in the Hawthorne factory were used as guinea pigs. One day the lighting in the work area for one group was improved dramatically while the other group's lighting remained unchanged. The researchers were surprised to find that the more highly illuminated workers' productivity improved dramatically when compared with the control group. The employees' working conditions were changed in other ways too (working hours, rest breaks and so on), and in all cases their productivity improved when a change was made. Indeed, their productivity even improved when the lights were dimmed again. By the time that everything had been returned to the way it was before the changes began, productivity at the factory was at its highest level ever. Absenteeism had plummeted.

The experimenters concluded that it was not the changes in physical conditions that were affecting the workers' productivity. Rather, it was the social conditions, the fact that someone was actually concerned about their workplace, and the opportunities that this gave the workers to discuss changes in their environment before they took place.

A crucial element in Mayo's findings was the effect that working in groups had on the individual. At one time he wrote:

> The desire to stand well with one's fellows, the so-called
> human instinct of association, easily outweighs the merely
> individual interest and the logic of reasoning upon which so
> many spurious principles of management are based.

Later in his life he added:

> The working group as a whole actually determined the
> output of individual workers by reference to a standard that
> represented the group conception (rather than management's)
> of a fair day's work. This standard was rarely, if ever, in
> accord with the standards of the efficiency engineers.

One leading member of the research team, Fritz Roethlisberger, wrote:

> The Hawthorne researchers became more and more
> interested in the informal employee groups, which tend to
> form within the formal organisation of the company, and
> which are not likely to be represented in the organisation
> chart. They became interested in the beliefs and creeds
> which have the effect of making each individual feel an
> integral part of the group.

Another of Mayo's theories was that conflict between managers and workers was inevitable as long as workers were ruled by "the logic of sentiment" and managers by the "logic of cost and efficiency". Only when each party appreciated the position of the other (through discussion and compromise) could conflict be avoided.

Recommended reading

Gillespie, G., *Manufacturing Knowledge, A History of the Hawthorne Experiments*, CUP, 1991

Mayo, E., *The Human Problems of an Industrial Civilisation*, Macmillan, 1933

Mayo, E., *The Social Problems of an Industrial Civilisation*, Harvard University Press, 1945

Roethlisberger, F.J. and Dickson, W.J., *Management and the Worker*, Harvard University Press, 1939

Hierarchy of needs

The hierarchy of needs is an idea associated almost entirely with one man, Abraham Maslow, the most influential anthropologist ever to have worked in industry. New York-born Maslow did anthropological research among the Blackfoot Indians in Alberta, Canada, before working in industry. He subsequently became professor of psychology at Brandeis University in Massachusetts.

The hierarchy of needs is a theory about the way in which people are motivated. It is directly relevant to the way in which companies motivate their employees and get the best out of them. Maslow first presented his theory in a paper ("A Theory of Human Motivation") published in the *Psychological Review* in 1943. In it he postulated that human needs fall into five different categories. Needs in the lower categories have to be satisfied before needs in the higher ones can act as motivators. Thus a violinist who is starving cannot be motivated to play Mozart, and a shop worker without a lunch break is less productive in the afternoon than one with a lunch break.

The theory arose out of a sense that classic economics was not giving managers much help because it failed to take into account the complexity of human motivation. Maslow himself wrote:

> *What conditions of work, what kinds of work, what kinds of management, and what kinds of reward or pay will help human stature to grow healthy, to its fuller and fullest stature? Classic economic theory, based as it is on an inadequate theory of human motivation, could be revolutionised by accepting the results of higher human needs, including the impulse to self-actualisation and the love for the highest values.*

Whole industries exist to satisfy the needs in Maslow's five categories.

- **Physiological needs:** hunger, thirst, sex and sleep. Food and drinks manufacturers operate to satisfy needs in this area, as do prostitutes and tobacco growers.
- **Safety needs:** job security, protection from harm and the avoidance of risk. At this level an individual's thoughts turn to

insurance, burglar alarms and savings deposits.

- **Social needs:** the affection of family and friendship. These include weddings, sophisticated restaurants and telecommunications.
- **Esteem needs** (also called ego needs), divided into internal needs, such as self-respect and sense of achievement, and external needs, such as status and recognition. Industries focused on this level include the sports industry and activity holidays.
- **Self-actualisation,** famously described by Maslow as: "A musician must make music, an artist must paint, a poet must write, if he is to be ultimately happy. What a man can be, he must be. This need we may call self-actualisation." This involves doing things such as going to art galleries, climbing mountains and writing novels. The theatre, cinema and music industries are all focused on this level. Self-actualisation is different from the other levels of need in at least one respect. It is never finished, never fully satisfied. It is, as Shakespeare put it, "as if increase of appetite grows by what it feeds on".

An individual's position in the hierarchy is constantly shifting as his or her needs shift. Any single act may satisfy needs at different levels. Thus having a drink at a bar with a friend may be satisfying both a thirst and a need for friendship (levels one and three). Single industries can also be aimed at satisfying needs at different levels. For example, a hotel provides food to satisfy level one, a restaurant to satisfy level three and special weekend tours of interesting sites to satisfy level five.

The hierarchy is not absolute. It is affected by the general environment in which the individual lives. The extent to which social needs are met in the workplace, for instance, varies according to culture. In Japan the corporate organisation is an important source of a man's sense of belonging (although not of a woman's); in the West it is much less so.

A brief history

Maslow was described by Peter Drucker, a widely respected business academic, as "the father of humanist psychology". But Drucker took issue with the hierarchy of needs. He wrote:

> *What Maslow did not see is that a want changes in the act of being satisfied ... as a want approaches satiety, its capacity to reward, and with it its power as an incentive, diminishes fast. But its capacity to deter, to create dissatisfaction, to act as a disincentive, rapidly increases.*

Maslow considered authoritarianism to be an aberration. The authoritarian characteristic, he said, "is the most important single disease afflicting man today – far more important than medical illnesses ... the most widespread of all diseases ... pandemic ... even in the United States, even in this classroom". People who achieve self-actualisation, he maintained, are democratic in outlook, not authoritarian.

Most of Maslow's prescriptions for business are based on democratic principles. One of his early disciples was a Californian company called NLS. In the early 1960s it dismantled its assembly line and replaced it with production teams of six or seven workers. Each team was responsible for the entire production process, and they worked in areas that they decorated according to their own taste. A host of other innovations (such as dispensing with time cards) revolutionised the company without any loss of productivity and with a considerable increase in employee morale.

On occasions Maslow's theory moved into philosophy and (almost) into religion. He once wrote:

> One's only rival is one's own potentialities. One's only failure is failing to live up to one's own possibilities. In this sense every man can be a king and must therefore be treated like a king.

Failing to use your talents is not a sin against your religion, it is a sin against yourself. (See also Theories X and Y, page 223.)

Recommended reading

Hoffman, E., *The Right to be Human, a Biography of Abraham Maslow*, Crucible Press (UK), 1989
Maslow, A., "A Theory of Human Motivation", *Psychological Review*, Vol. 50, 1943
Maslow, A., *Motivation and Personality*, Harper and Row, 1954
Stees, R.M. and Porter, L.W., *Motivation and Work Behaviour*, (5th edition), McGraw-Hill, 1991
www.ozemail.com.au/~tlc/needs-nf.html – The Maslow Need Hierarchy

Innovation

Innovation is "a creative idea that has been made to work", writes David Hussey in *The Innovation Challenge*. "It can be as basic as a procedural change in a distribution system or as complex as entry into a whole new market."

Everybody knows an innovative company when they see one. In lists of such companies the same names come up again and again – 3M, Hewlett-Packard, General Electric, Sony – companies where continual innovation has produced far higher returns than an ordinary business investment. 3M's progressive policy on innovation commits it to earning 30% of its revenue from products that have been brought to market within the previous four years. The company allows its employees to spend 15% of their time pursuing ideas that they think have potential.

There are two fundamental views of what it takes to manage innovation. One, held by people like Clayton Christensen of the Harvard Business School, is that innovation is nurtured in special and highly creative environments. These environments, Christensen believes, are most easily created in small companies.

> *There is something about the way that decisions get made in successful organisations that sows the seeds of eventual failure ... Many large companies adopt a strategy of waiting until new markets are "large enough to be interesting". But this is not often a successful strategy.*

The other view is that any company, however big or cumbersome, can make itself more innovative in a more mundane way, by changing its management structures, systems and practices. This is the "it doesn't take a genius to do ingenious things" school of thought.

The first thing companies do if they want to follow this approach is to encourage innovation systematically, to trawl through all types of change and assess them for potentially profitable business opportunities. Then they encourage the sorts of people who are driven to succeed at new things. As Peter Drucker has pointed out, creativity is not the limiting factor: "There are more ideas in any organisation, including business, than can possibly be put to use." The issue is how to manage the creativity, the innovation, so that it creates economic value.

The American National Research Council found from its surveys that the main ingredients enabling the United States to capitalise on innovation, which it does better than most countries, are "sustained research leadership, a favourable business environment, increasingly flexible human resources, and new forms of co-operation between academia, industry and government. These ingredients are increasingly interactive and mutually reinforcing".

In his book *Innovation and Entrepreneurship, Practice and Principles*, Peter Drucker wrote that there are seven areas where companies should look for opportunities to be innovative. The first four are internal to the company and the last three are external.

1 The unexpected success that is rarely dissected to see how it occurred.
2 Any incongruity between what actually happens and what was expected to happen.
3 Any inadequacy in a business process that is taken for granted.
4 A change in industry or market structure that takes everybody by surprise.
5 Demographic changes caused by things like wars, migrations, medical developments (such as the birth-control pill).
6 Changes in perception and fashion brought about by changes in the economy.
7 Changes in awareness caused by new knowledge.

A brief history

Innovation has been a subject of great fascination for centuries. At the end of the 1500s Sir Francis Bacon wrote: "He that will not apply new remedies must expect new evils: for time is the greatest innovator."

John Jewkes, author of *The Sources of Invention*, reviewing the history of the subject, wrote:

> *There seems to be no subject in which traditional and uncritical stories, casual rumours, sweeping generalisations, myths and conflicting records more widely abound, in which every man seems to be interested and in which, perhaps because miracles seem to be the natural order, scepticism is at a discount. Perhaps no-one can hope entirely to escape the mild mesmerising influence of the subject.*

From their research, P. Ranganath Nayak and John Ketteringham found that there were seven myths surrounding the process of business innovation.

1 That commercial breakthroughs come from ideas that nobody has had before.
2 That inventors make breakthroughs.
3 That if you build a better mousetrap, the world will beat a path to your doorstep.
4 That all the great ideas come from little guys.
5 That big success requires big resources.
6 That the commercial breakthrough requires a special sort of environment.
7 That breakthroughs always respond to an unfulfilled need.

Many commentators have divided innovation into two parts: invention and implementation. The old idea was that invention and implementation followed each other in an unhurried sequence. An economist, Alfred Marshall, once wrote:

> The full importance of an epoch-making idea is often not perceived in the generation in which it is made ... a new discovery is seldom fully effective for practical purposes till many minor improvements and subsidiary discoveries have gathered themselves around it.

Although this may have been true at the end of the 19th century, it is not so today. In the online business world, things happen at such a speed that the "minor improvements and subsidiary discoveries" take place almost at the same time as the epoch-making idea itself.

Another big change in business innovation has been pointed out by James Brian Quinn, a professor of management at Dartmouth College and co-author of a classic textbook, The Strategy Process. "Most of today's innovation is not in products, but in services and software," he wrote in 1999. "These process changes (induced by software) are lowering needed innovation times, investments and risks, by 60–90%."

The central importance of innovation to business and general economic success is now widely acknowledged by governments as well as by business. In the British government's 1999 budget report (known as the Red Book) it wrote that:

Innovation and R&D are central to technical progress, which is a key driver of long-run growth. The process of innovation encompasses all aspects of firm performance, from R&D, through to new processes and products, to a culture of continuous training and improvement. Failure to understand this process was a key weakness in traditional analyses of growth.

The British government was clearly a full convert to what *The Economist* has called "the industrial religion of the late 20th century", even to the extent of embracing the language that goes with it: "key drivers", "processes" and "culture of continuous improvement". It could have been written for the British chancellor by a management consultant. Indeed, it probably was.

Recommended reading

Christensen, C., *The Innovator's Dilemma*, Harvard Business School Press, 1997

De Bono, E., *Practical Thinking*, Jonathan Cape, 1971

Drucker, P., *Innovation and Entrepreneurship, Practice and Principles*, Harper & Row, 1985

Drucker, P., "The Discipline of Innovation", *Harvard Business Review*, May-June 1985 (reprinted in *Harvard Business Review*, November-December 1998)

Hussey, D. (ed.), *The Innovation Challenge*, John Wiley, 1997

Jewkes, J., *The Sources of Invention*, Macmillan, 1961

Ranganath Nayak, P. and Ketteringham, J., *Breakthroughs* (based on an international study of innovation by Arthur D. Little), Rawson Associates, 1986

Quinn, J.B., "Managing Innovation: Controlled Chaos", *Harvard Business Review*, May-June 1985

Takeuchi, H. and Nonaka, I., "The New Product Development Game", *Harvard Business Review*, January-February 1986

Valéry, N., "Innovation in Industry", survey for *The Economist*, February 20th 1999

Intrapreneurship

One definition says that intrapreneurship is "the introduction and implementation of a significant innovation for the firm by one or more employees working within an established organisation". It is the blossoming of the entrepreneurial spirit inside a large organisation. An intrapreneur is an intra-corporate entrepreneur, one who works as an employee of a corporation.

Intrapreneurship offers large organisations the hope that they can remain entrepreneurial long after they have ceased to be run by entrepreneurs. (See "How can big companies keep the entrepreneurial spirit alive?" by B. Harris *et al* in the *Harvard Business Review*, November-December 1995.)

Small companies and large companies encourage intrapreneurs in different ways. In smaller companies, intrapreneurship has more to do with the informal relationships that build up between individuals within the firm; in larger companies it has to be systematically encouraged by formal procedures. It also has to be encouraged for a long time. In early 1999, *The Economist* said: "All big innovations need to be championed and nurtured for long periods, sometimes up to 25 years".

The International Management Centre's website lists a few questions that employees should ask themselves if they want to know whether they are intrapreneurial or not.

1 Do you get excited about what you are doing at work?
2 Do you think about new business ideas while driving to work or taking a shower?
3 Do you get into trouble from time to time for doing things which exceed your authority?
4 Are you able to keep your ideas under cover, suppressing the urge to tell everybody about them until you have tested them and produced a plan for implementation?
5 Have you successfully pushed through bleak times, when something on which you were working looked as if it might fail?
6 Do you have more than your share of both fans and critics?
7 Can you consider trying to overcome a natural perfectionist tendency to do all the work yourself and share responsibility for your ideas with a team?

8 Would you be willing to give up some of your salary in exchange for the chance to try out your business idea, if the rewards for success were adequate?

Anyone who answers Yes more often than No could (possibly) be an intrapreneur.

A brief history

The selling of the Post-It note (see Championing, page 27) by Spence Silver, an employee of 3M, is one of the classic and most quoted examples of intrapreneurship. 3M has been particularly successful at encouraging intrapreneurs. It maintains that the first thing you have to do is to create a corporate culture which permits ideas to blossom. "You have to kiss a lot of frogs to find the prince," the company told *The Economist*. "But remember, one prince can pay for a lot of frogs."

Another way in which companies have tried to create intrapreneurs is through what are known as "skunkworks". These are modelled on the Lockheed aircraft company's secret research-cum-production facility where, in the late 1940s, staff were removed from the corporate bureaucracy and encouraged to ignore standard procedures in the hope that they would come up with innovative products. They did so, in sufficient quantities for the idea to be copied by several other large companies, including IBM. Big Blue used it to break free from its suffocating mainframe mentality and join the world of the PC, at a time when many of its rivals were unable to make the switch.

In the 1990s large companies became ever keener to inject intrapreneurship into their organisations as they saw the advantages of being small increase with the spread of information technology. Martin Sorrell, chairman of WPP, a large multinational group of advertising agencies, told the *McKinsey Quarterly*:

> Every company that is ambitious wants to dominate its
> industry, and therefore become very large. At the same time,
> every chairman and CEO is worried about size and the
> resultant lack of speed of response, bureaucracy, arrogance,
> and complacency. As a result, all companies want the
> power of size and the entrepreneurial spirit and motivation
> of a small company.

Bell Atlantic introduced a special intrapreneurial programme into its staff training, and the Ford Motor Company, one of the last bastions of the corporate rule-book, also set out recently to make its employees feel like entrepreneurs. When Jacques Nasser, an Australian of Lebanese origin whose early working years had been spent running (and starting) a range of small businesses, became boss in the late 1990s he initiated a training programme. Employees were sent on a three-day workshop, after which they had to come up with a significant new cost saving (or revenue source) for the company within 100 days.

Recommended reading

Block, Z. and MacMillan, I.C., *Corporate Venturing: Creating New Businesses within the Firm*, Harvard Business School Press, 1993

Drucker, P., *Innovation and Entrepreneurship: Practices and Principles*, Heineman, 1985

Pinchot, Gifford III, *Intrapreneuring*, Harper and Row, 1995

Hamel, G., "The challenge today: changing the rules of the game", *Business Strategy Review*, Summer 1998

Just-in-time

When first introduced in Japan in the 1970s, just-in-time (JIT) marked a radical new approach to the manufacturing process. It cut waste by supplying parts only as and when the process required them. The old system became known (by contrast) as the just-in-case system; inventory was held for every possible eventuality, just in case it came about.

JIT eliminated the need for each stage in the production process to hold buffer stocks, which resulted in huge savings. It was not only expensive to hold unused accumulated inventory, it also required time and effort to store and manage it.

JIT had other advantages. It involved the workforce much more directly in controlling their own inventory needs, and it allowed a variety of models to be produced on the same assembly line simultaneously. Before its introduction, assembly lines had been able to cope with only one model at a time. To produce another model required closure of the line and expensive retooling.

At the heart of JIT lies the *kanban*, the Japanese word for card. In this case it refers to the card that is sent to reorder a standard quantity of parts as and when they have been used up in a manufacturing process. Before JIT, batches of, say, X + Y parts would be ordered at a time, and the *kanban* would be sent for a replacement order when only Y parts were left. Y was precisely the quantity needed to carry on until the new parts arrived. With JIT only Y parts were ordered, and the *kanban* was sent off as soon as the new order arrived. It thus eliminated, in effect, the need to hold X parts in permanent storage.

Over the years, JIT came to have hung on to it all the trappings of an almost mystical philosophy. In their book *Operations Management*, Roberta Russell and Bernard Taylor describe how it evolved:

> If you produce only what you need when you need it, then
> there is no room for error. For JIT to work, many
> fundamental elements must be in place – steady production,
> flexible resources, extremely high quality, no machine
> breakdowns, reliable suppliers, quick machine set-ups, and
> lots of discipline to maintain the other elements. Just-in-
> time is both a philosophy and an integrated system for
> production management that evolved slowly through a

trial-and-error process over a span of more than 15 years.
There was no masterplan or blueprint for JIT.

JIT thus sat at the centre of the total quality movement (see page 225) and of the flexible manufacturing techniques that were the essence of lean production (see page 136), the name given originally to the manufacturing system that the Toyota company rapidly developed into one of the most efficient in the world.

A brief history

A Toyota employee, Taiichi Ohno, is accredited with adopting the first JIT manufacturing method at one of the Japanese car company's plants in the early 1970s. It arose out of two things.

- Japan's concern to improve the relationship of the cost of its production to its quality. At the time, Japanese companies were notorious for producing shoddy goods, and they were unable to benefit in the same way as American automobile manufacturers from vast economies of scale (see page 76).
- The Japanese tradition of continuous improvement (called *kaizen*, see page 126).

Some people say that the idea predates the Toyota experience, and that it began in the 1950s when Japanese shipbuilders were able to take advantage of overcapacity in the steel industry to demand delivery of steel as and when they required it. Some shipbuilders became so skilled at this that they were able to cut their inventories from 30-days worth to three-days worth.

The system soon became widely copied, both inside and outside Japan. There was some initial scepticism in the United States, however, until companies like Hewlett-Packard (where it became known as "stockless production") began to demonstrate that the system could be transplanted successfully into other cultures. One study found that American firms that introduced JIT gained over the next five years (on average) a 70% reduction in inventory, a 50% reduction in labour costs and an 80% reduction in space requirements.

Recommended reading

Cheng, T.C.E. and Podolsky, S., *Just-in-Time Manufacturing*, Chapman and Hall (2nd edition), 1996

Hirano, H., *JIT Factory Revolution*, Productivity Press, 1988

Russell, R.S. and Taylor, B.W., *Operations Management*, Prentice Hall (2nd edition), 1998

Schonberger, R.J., *World Class Manufacturing: the Lessons of Simplicity Applied*, The Free Press, 1986

Womack, J., Jones, D. and Roos, D., *The Machine that Changed the World*, Macmillan, 1990

Kaizen

Kaizen is one of a batch of oriental ideas seized upon by western companies in the 1980s when it was thought that Japan contained almost all the wisdom there was to know about management. Like several other Japanese business concepts of the time, it began with the letter K – like *keiretsu* (see page 128) and *kanban* (see Just-in-Time, page 123), for instance. As Kellogg, Kodak, Kraft and Kit-Kat have proven, the letter K adds a peculiar power to a name.

"When applied to the workplace," says Masaaki Imai, an author whose 1986 book on *kaizen* sparked much of the western interest, "*kaizen* means continuous improvement involving everyone, managers and workers alike." Imai subsequently became chairman of the Kaizen Institute, a network of consultants around the world dedicated to helping clients to "sustain continual improvement in all aspects of their enterprises".

Kaizen has also been translated as "refinement", the process by which a rough diamond gradually gets smoothed into a high-quality gemstone. In Japanese culture, the idea of refinement has a particular significance. It is not, for example, considered to be copying to take someone else's idea and then to refine it for yourself. This is considered to be a celebration of your environment.

Kaizen has three underlying principles:

- that human resources are a company's most important asset;
- that processes must evolve by gradual improvement rather than by radical change; and
- that improvement must be based on a quantitative evaluation of the performance of different processes. (See also Total quality management, page 225. TQM is a system designed for implementing *kaizen*.)

A brief history

Kaizen lost some of its shine with the slowdown of the Japanese industrial bulldozer. Books like *Kaisha, the Japanese Corporation*, by James Abegglen and George Stalk, two Tokyo-based consultants with the Boston Consulting Group, helped to dispel the myth. "The range of competence among Japan's companies should not be overlooked," wrote the authors, a comment that was reinforced by the financial troubles of many Japanese household names in the late 1990s.

Also influential in the decline of the *kaizen* idea was the new-found emphasis in the 1990s on the speed of change and on the need for firms to "morph" in double-quick time to seize the opportunities presented by e-commerce (see page 74) and other developments in information technology. It was hard to fit the steady deliberation of *kaizen* into such an environment. *Kaizen's* gradualism no longer seemed to suit the mood of the times.

Recommended reading

Abegglen, J.C. and Stalk, G., *Kaisha: the Japanese Corporation*, Basic Books, 1985

Cusumano, M.A., *Japan's Software Factories*, Oxford University Press, 1990

Imai, M., *Kaizen: the Key to Japan's Competitive Success*, McGraw-Hill, 1986

Imai, M., *Gemba Kaizen*, McGraw-Hill, 1997

Lewis, K.C., *Kaizen: The Right Approach to Continuous Improvement*, IFS International, 1995

www.kaizeninstitute.com/mo1.html – The Kaizen Institute

Keiretsu

Keiretsu is a Japanese word which, translated literally, means headless combine. It is the name given to a form of corporate structure in which a number of organisations link together, usually by taking small stakes in each other and usually as a result of having a close business relationship, often as suppliers to each other. The structure, frequently likened to a spider's web, was much admired in the 1990s as a way to defuse the traditionally adversarial relationship between buyer and supplier. If you own a bit of your supplier, reinforced sometimes by your supplier owning a bit of you, the theory says that you are more likely to reach a way of working that is of mutual benefit to you both than if your relationship is at arm's length.

American trade officials, however, disliked Japan's *keiretsu* because they saw them as a restraint of trade. Jeffrey Garten, once under-secretary of commerce in charge of international trade and then dean of the Yale School of Management, said that a *keiretsu* restrains trade "because there is a very strong preference to do business only with someone in that family".

A brief history

By the mid-1990s the *keiretsu* concept was in vogue. Jeffrey Dyer wrote in the *Harvard Business Review* that Chrysler had created "an American *keiretsu*". The company's relationship with its suppliers, which were reduced in number from 2,500 in 1989 to 1,140 in 1996, had improved to such an extent, claimed Dyer, that "the two sides now strive together to find ways to lower the costs of making cars and to share the savings".

In the UK Richard Branson, founder of the Virgin group, wrote in *The Economist* that "at the centre of our *keiretsu* brand will be a global airline and city-centre megastores acting like flagships for the brand around the world". In *The New Yorker* in 1997 Ken Auletta mapped out the intricate *keiretsu* that he claimed was being woven by six of the world's mightiest media, entertainment and software giants: Microsoft, Disney, Time Warner, News Corporation, TCI and GE·NBC. Meanwhile, closer to the original home of the *keiretsu*, the South Korean economic miracle was being fired by the country's *chaebol*, industrial groupings modelled closely on the *keiretsu*.

The American *keiretsu*, however, were fundamentally different from the Japanese model. In Japan they were regulated by specific laws, and they were structured in such a way that co-operation between them was almost compulsory. Outside Japan, the word *keiretsu* became attached to any loose network of alliances between more than two organisations. Moreover, the American companies' reasons for linking together were slightly different from those of traditional Japanese groups such as Mitsubishi or Sumitomo. The Americans were joining forces, wrote Auletta, "to create a safety net of sorts, because technology is changing so rapidly that no one can be sure which technology or which business will be ascendant". In the process, he predicted that the *keiretsu* would become "the next corporate order".

Recommended reading

Auletta, K., "American Keiretsu", *The New Yorker*, October 1997

Dyer, J.H., "How Chrysler Created an American Keiretsu", *Harvard Business Review*, July-August 1996

Ferguson, C.H., "Computers and the Coming of the US Keiretsu", *Harvard Business Review*, July-August 1990

Miyashita, K. and Russell, D., *Keiretsu: Inside the Hidden Japanese Conglomerates*, McGraw-Hill, 1994

Knowledge management

In 1988 Peter Drucker, the founder of modern management science, wrote:

> The typical business [of the future] will be knowledge-based, an organisation composed largely of specialists who direct and discipline their own performance through feedback from colleagues, customers and headquarters. For this reason it will be what I call an information-based organisation.

In such a business, the management of knowledge and information becomes an important skill.

"Business today", echoed Charles Handy, the UK's leading management writer, in 1992, "depends largely on intellectual property, which resides inalienably in the hearts and heads of individuals." Both writers were reflecting a broadening realisation that companies had moved far from Victorian times, when they were (as Handy put it) "properties with tangible assets worked by hands whose time owners bought". But the legislation and attitudes that governed them had not moved in line with the change.

Knowledge, which existed either in the heads and hearts of its employees or in formal databases, patents, copyrights and so on, was increasingly seen as a company's most valuable asset. Lester Thurow, an American management professor, went so far as to suggest in a 1997 article in the *Harvard Business Review* that intellectual property rights had become more important than manufacturing products or dealing in commodities. Once companies realised this for themselves they became aware of the need to find out how to manage this knowledge, how to use it systematically to create extra value. This was not something that they had addressed systematically in the past.

Information technology helped them in their attempt to introduce good knowledge-management practices. Developments in IT advanced the science immeasurably. Data warehousing (the centralising of information in vast electronic databases), for example, enabled companies to be much more sophisticated and customer-oriented in their business. At last, the left hand knew what the right hand was doing;

the marketing department knew who was already a customer of the company, and for what product or service.

Knowledge management is seen not only as the key to the creation of business wealth but also, increasingly, as the key to the creation of national wealth. In the British government's 1998 White Paper on the competitiveness of the nation, it said: "Our success depends on how well we exploit our most valuable assets: our knowledge, skills and creativity ... they are at the heart of a modern knowledge-driven economy."

There are several things that can be done to improve a company's knowledge management.

- **Capturing information.** All employees should be made aware of the ways in which knowledge can be of use to the organisation. The organisation should ensure that it is not suddenly bereft of vital information when an important individual moves to another employer.
- **Generating ideas.** All employees should be made aware that not all good ideas are rocket science that only come out of an R&D department. Everybody should be encouraged to come up with new ideas, through ideas boxes, for instance, or by gaining rewards for ideas that make or save money for the company.
- **Storing information.** Data warehouses should be structured so that the information in them can be accessed by everybody in the organisation and recycled in ways that are valuable to the organisation.
- **Distributing information.** Organisations must persuade people to give information to others when it is for the benefit of the business as a whole. For too long information in organisations has been seen primarily as power. As such, it has too often been retained by managers for their own personal power games.

Some say that the best way to make people share knowledge is to make them work together in the same room. When teams are put together to carry out specific tasks, they are often made to spend time together in close proximity. Virtual teams, connected by e-mail and phone, do not have the same dynamics.

Recommended reading
Nonaka, I. and Takeuchi, H., *The Knowledge Creating Company*, Oxford University Press, 1995

Leadership

Leadership is "one of the most observed and least understood phenomena on earth" wrote one man in a position to know. In business writing, there have been three approaches to the subject:

- the nature and behaviour of leaders;
- the nature and behaviour of those who are led; and
- the structure of the organisation in which the leading takes place.

Most is written about the first of these strands. There is a visceral fascination with leaders and their character, and with the great issue that surrounds them: can leaders be made or can they only be born?

First, though, what are the qualities of a leader? Field Marshal Montgomery thought that a leader "must have infectious optimism, and the determination to persevere in the face of difficulties. He must also radiate confidence, even when he himself is not too certain of the outcome". Henri Fayol, an early French writer on management, said that the leader's task is "thinking out a plan and ensuring its success". It is, he added, "one of the keenest satisfactions for an intelligent man to experience".

David Ogilvy, founder of an advertising agency, Ogilvy & Mather, and himself a leader of some quality, thought:

> Great leaders almost always exude self-confidence. They are
> never petty. They are never buck-passers. They pick
> themselves up after defeat ... They do not suffer from the
> crippling need to be universally loved ... The great leaders I
> have known have been curiously complicated men.

This view of the leader as a complicated personality is borne out by the characters of some undeniably great leaders, such as Napoleon and Winston Churchill, and by the fact that up to 60% of presidents of the United States and prime ministers of the UK lost their fathers before they were 14.

However, the leadership of people like Alfred P. Sloan, the legendary boss of General Motors, owed more to the structure and systems that they put in place in their organisations (based in Sloan's case on the theory of "decentralisation and co-ordinated control") than they did on the personality of the leader. Henry Ford II was also a man whose success in revitalising the family firm after the second world war depended on his reorganisation of the company. The man himself was a jet-setting playboy who rarely met the David Ogilvy standards of a great leader. The same could be said of many other bosses of big corporations around the world.

The leading management thinker on leadership in the later years of the 20th century was Warren Bennis, a professor at the University of Southern California. He said that successful leaders follow an almost universal principle of management "as true for orchestra conductors, army generals, football coaches, and school superintendents as for corporate executives". He found that the vast majority of successful leaders were white males who remained married to the same person all their lives. When they came to head an organisation, successful leaders "paid attention to what was going on, determined what part of the events at hand would be important for the future of the organisation, set a new direction, and concentrated the attention of everyone in the organisation on it".

In *Leaders, The Strategies for Taking Charge*, Bennis lists four competencies that leaders need to develop:

- forming a vision which provides people with a bridge to the future;
- giving meaning to that vision through communication;
- building trust, "the lubrication that makes it possible for organisations to work";
- searching for self-knowledge and self-regard. In this context, Bennis says: "I think a lot of the leaders I've spoken to give expression to their feminine side. Many male leaders are almost bisexual in their ability to be open and reflective ... Gender is not the determining factor."

The worst problem for leaders, says Bennis, is "early success. There's no opportunity to learn from adversity and problems".

A brief history

Bruce Henderson, founder of the Boston Consulting Group, defined a way of distinguishing leadership from management. He said that "the management function deals with what the organisation ought to do. The leadership function deals with the motivation of the organisation to do that which it ought to do". Warren Bennis echoes this distinction by saying, "Managers do things right. Leaders do the right thing."

Abraham Zaleznik, in an influential article in the *Harvard Business Review*, argued that "because leaders and managers are basically different, the conditions favourable to one may be inimical to the growth of the other". In other words, a long career as a manager may not be the best training for a leader. But this is the training that most leaders get.

The nature of leadership has been discussed since time immemorial. In perhaps the most famous book on the subject, *The Prince*, written in Florence in the 1520s, Niccolo Machiavelli set out his ideas about what a prince must do to survive and prosper, surrounded as he inevitably will be by general human malevolence. Dedicated to Lorenzo de Medici, the book draws on examples from history, of Alexander the Great and of the German city states, to teach its readers some eternal lessons in leadership. Many a corporate chief executive keeps a copy by his bedside.

The ideas of Machiavelli were entertainingly set in a business context by Alistair McAlpine in the 1980s. Machiavelli's comment that "Some princes, in order to hold on to their states securely, have disarmed their subjects, some have kept their subject towns divided, and some have fostered animosity against themselves" was developed by McAlpine into three styles of management structure.

1 In one, the power of decision-making is removed from line management and kept firmly in the hands of a small clique at head office.
2 In the second, one branch office is played off against another in "what is called by some 'creative tension'".
3 Lastly, there is the style in which senior managers are kept in a permanent state of fear. The leader is always "digging at them with words, driving them with threats, always leaving them wondering if they will still have employment the next day".

(See also Vision, page 238.)

Recommended reading

Bennis, W., *Leaders: The Strategies for Taking Charge*, Harper & Row, 1986
Bennis, W. and Nanus, B., *Leaders*, Harper & Row, 1985
Bennis, W., *Organising Genius*, Nicholas Brealey, 1997

Burns, J.M., *Leadership*, Harper & Row, 1978

Kotter, J.P., *The Leadership Factor*, Free Press, 1982

Goleman, D., "What Makes a Leader?", *Harvard Business Review*, November-December 1998

Green, P., *Alexander the Great*, Frederick A. Prager, 1970

Jay, A., *Management and Machiavelli*, Penguin, 1970

Machiavelli, N., *The Prince*, 1527, Florence

McAlpine, A., *The New Machiavelli*, Aurum Press, 1997

Mintzberg, H., "Covert Leadership: Notes on Managing Professionals", *Harvard Business Review*, November-December 1998

Tichy, N., *Transformational Leadership*, John Wiley, 1984

Zaleznik, A., *Human Dilemmas of Leadership*, Harper & Row, 1966

Zaleznik, A., "Managers and Leaders: Are they Different?", *Harvard Business Review*, May-June, 1977

Zaleznik, A., "Real Work", *Harvard Business Review*, January-February 1989

Lean production

Lean production is the name given to a group of highly efficient manufacturing techniques developed (mainly by large Japanese companies) in the 1980s and early 1990s. Lean production was seen as the third step in an historical progression, which took industry from the age of the craftsman through the methods of mass production (see page 148) and into an era that combined the best of both. It has been described as "the most fundamental change to occur since mass production was brought to full development by Henry Ford early in the 20th century".

The methods of lean production are said to combine the flexibility and quality of craft production with the low costs of mass production. In lean-production systems a manufacturer's employees are organised in teams. Within each team a worker is expected to be able to do all the tasks required of the team. These tasks are less narrowly specialised than those demanded of the worker in a mass-production system, and this variety enables the worker to escape from the soul-destroying repetition of the pure assembly line.

With lean production, components are delivered to each team's work station just-in-time (see page 123), and every worker is encouraged to stop production when a fault is discovered. This is a critical distinction from the classic assembly-line process. Stopping an assembly line is expensive and to be avoided at all costs. Often it is only the line foreman who is allowed to stop it. Faulty products are put to one side to be dealt with later, and a large stock of spares is kept on hand so that faulty components can be replaced immediately without causing hold-ups. The problem with such a system is that workers on the assembly line learn nothing, so the faults often persist. Workers are not encouraged to look back and find the source of the fault, and then to be involved in its correction.

When a lean production system is first introduced, stoppages generally increase while problems are ironed out. Gradually, however, there are fewer stoppages and fewer problems. In the end, a mature lean-production line stops much less frequently than a mature mass-production assembly line.

Lean production gains in another way too. In typical assembly-line operations, design is farmed out to specialist outsiders or to a separate team of insiders. Gaining feedback from both the production-line workers and the component suppliers is a long and awkward process.

With lean production, designers work hand-in-hand with production workers and suppliers. There is a continuous two-way interchange. Snags can be ironed out immediately and machine tools adapted on the hoof. With the assembly-line model, the communication is linear.

A brief history

Lean production methods have been introduced by many companies without sacrificing economies of scale (see page 76). Japanese car manufacturers have achieved unit costs of production well below those of more traditionally organised European and American manufacturers with twice their volume. These same Japanese companies have also been leaders in the speed and efficiency of new product design, a vital skill in a world where time to market is an important competitive lever.

According to Michael Cusumano, the high productivity achieved by the lean production methods of Japan's car companies depends, not as some have maintained on a peculiarity of Japanese culture or of Japanese workers, but on technology and management. He says:

> The methods challenged fundamental assumptions about
> mass production. These consisted of revisions in American
> and European equipment, production techniques, and
> labour and supplier policies introduced primarily in the
> 1950s and 1960s when total Japanese manufacturing volumes
> and volumes per model were extremely low by US or
> European standards.

Lean production methods can now be found in factories all over the world. A striking success story is that of a British engineering company, British Aerospace. In the five years to the end of 1998 it was the best-performing company in the UK in terms of its total return to shareholders. It achieved this in part by shedding non-core businesses, such as the Rover car company, and in part by introducing into its core defence and aerospace businesses the lean production ideas that Rover had picked up from Japanese car manufacturers in the 1980s.

Recommended reading

Cusumano, M., "Manufacturing innovation: lessons from the Japanese auto industry", *Sloan Management Review*, Vol. 30, 1988

Womack, J.P., Jones, D.T. and Roos, D., *The Machine That Changed the World*, Maxwell Macmillan, 1990

The learning organisation

The idea of the organisation as a living, learning entity was developed by Chris Argyris and Donald Schon in their 1978 book *Organisational Learning*. Learning by the people within an organisation becomes learning by the organisation itself. The changes in people's attitudes are reflected in changes in the formal and informal rules that govern the organisation's behaviour.

A learning organisation, wrote Peter Senge in *The Fifth Discipline*, the book that popularised the idea, is "an organisation that is continually expanding its capacity to create its future". It is continuously learning new ways of doing things and also (necessarily) involved in a continuous process of unlearning, of forgetting old ways of doing things.

Organisations work as a set of interconnected subsystems, says Senge, so decisions made in one part of the business have implications for the other parts. Managers, therefore, need to embrace the complexity of organisations rather than embracing what he calls "the pervasive reductionalism" of western culture, whereby simple answers to complex questions are always sought. Senge says that a non-threatening dialogue needs to be carried out among the employees of an organisation in which some sort of consensus is reached as each employee comes to see the points of view of all the others, and begins to learn from them.

The idea of the learning organisation has been developed rather differently by Arie de Geus, a Dutchman who worked for Royal Dutch Shell for 38 years before becoming a visiting fellow at the London Business School. De Geus starts with a model of the company as a living thing. Like other living organisms, it exists in order to survive and to fulfil its potential. But in order to do this, organisms must be constantly learning how to adapt to their environment. Companies are no exception. They must become learning organisations that change and adapt to suit their changing business environment.

There are a number of radical consequences of thinking of companies as living organisms. Living beings, as opposed to dead things, have character and will and can make choices. In particular, they are:

- goal-oriented;
- self-aware – they know who is a member of the company (a subsidiary) and who is not (a supplier). Most importantly, the

shareholder is not a member of the living company, it is an external stakeholder, much like a trade union or a customer;
- subject to disease – the threat of a takeover, for instance, can damage a company's health; and
- mortal – eventually they die.

De Geus's work has fostered businessmen's interest in ecology, the study of how organisms relate to their environment. Living companies, like organisms, face a conflict between long-term evolution and short-term gain.

A brief history

Peter Senge, director of the Centre for Organisational Learning at MIT's Sloan School of Management, has studied how firms and organisations develop adaptive capabilities in a world of increasing complexity and rapid change. Senge's message is that organisations obtain competitive advantage from continuous learning, both individual and collective. The technology of the information age, however, is radically changing the way in which such learning takes place, and companies need to think through the implications of this for their own learning process. This almost invariably requires a radical restructuring.

De Geus argues that companies have not been particularly successful at adaptation. The life expectancy of most companies is short. Thousands and thousands are registered and liquidated every year. Even large, seemingly successful organisations have, according to de Geus, not been particularly good at learning to adapt.

Royal Dutch Shell dates back to the 1890s, and there are only about 40 large corporations around the world that pre-date it. But companies have the potential to live for centuries. In the UK the qualification for membership of one corporate club is that a company be more than 300 years old. A Swedish group, Stora, began life as a copper-mining company seven centuries ago, and Takatoshi Mitsui, who founded an eponymous drapery shop, died in 1694. His company has been through many adventures since, but the Mitsui group is still very much alive.

A good example of adaptation can be found at a Finnish company, Nokia. A few years ago it was a forest-products business making paper and pulp. It was sufficiently astute, however, to recognise that it was in a troubled industry with overcapacity. Somehow it sensed that mobile phones could be a growth business in the future, and it switched. It is now the biggest manufacturer of mobile phones in the world and one of the greatest creators of value in the 1990s.

The case of Nokia lends support to the Darwinian view of organisations, a view that was popular in the early 1990s. Organisations learn, it claimed, in order to survive in a world where the overriding principle is "survival of the fittest". Failures provide information which others can use to learn how to correct their ways.

Recommended reading

Argyris, C. and Schon, D.A., *Organisational Learning*, Addison-Wesley, 1978

De Geus, A., *The Living Company*, Harvard Business School Press, 1997

De Geus, A., "The Living Company", *Harvard Business Review*, March-April 1997

Senge, P., *The Fifth Discipline, the Art and Practice of the Learning Organisation*, Doubleday, 1990

Management by objectives

The idea of management by objectives (MBO), first outlined by Peter Drucker and then developed by his student, George Odiorne, was popular in the 1960s and 1970s. In his book *The Practice of Management*, published in 1954, Drucker outlined a number of priorities for the manager of the future. Top of the list was that he or she "must manage by objectives". Drucker's biographer, John Tarrant, reported in 1976 that Drucker said that he had first heard the term MBO used by Alfred Sloan, author of the influential *My Years with General Motors*.

With the benefit of hindsight, it may seem obvious that managers must have somewhere to go before they set out on a journey. But for many at the time it came as a blinding flash. Odiorne said:

> *Drucker has been a voice of sanity in graduate schools.*
> *Faculty members are still busy running mathematical*
> *models and measuring the distance between managers'*
> *eyeballs, but Drucker has always focused on what managers*
> *actually do.*

He also said that managers lose sight of their objectives because of something called "the activity trap". They get so involved in their current activities that they forget their original purpose. In some cases they become engrossed in this activity as a means of avoiding the uncomfortable truth about their organisation's condition.

A library of literature about MBO appeared soon after, much of it as unreadable then as it is today. Managers of the smallest business units were urged to follow the principles of MBO: first, determine the business's objectives; then plan how to achieve those objectives efficiently; and lastly implement that plan.

MBO urged that the planning process, traditionally done by a few high-level managers, should involve all members of the organisation. The plan, when it finally emerged, would then have the commitment of all of them. As the plan is implemented, MBO demands that the organisation should monitor a range of performance measures, designed to help it follow the right path towards its objectives. The plan must be modified when this monitoring suggests that it is no longer leading in the right direction.

One of the more fruitful outcomes of the MBO literature was a fresh analysis of objectives that soon came into common currency. It was known by its acronym – objectives, it said, must be SMART:

- ▰ Specific
- ▰ Measurable
- ▰ Achievable
- ▰ Realistic
- ▰ Time-related

One critic claimed that MBO encouraged organisations to tamper with their plans all the time, as and when they seemed no longer to be heading towards some immutable objective. This was often counter-productive, and many firms came to prefer the vague overall objectives of a mission statement (see page 154) to the firm, rigid ones demanded by MBO.

After a while, Drucker himself downplayed the significance of MBO. "MBO", he said, "is just another tool. It is not the great cure for management inefficiency ... Management by objectives works if you know the objectives: 90% of the time you don't." Drucker's central point is that management has to be all pervasive, and that it is primarily a human activity, not a mechanical or an economic one. Too much business activity still takes place without it.

A brief history

The idea of management by objectives received a boost when it was declared to be an integral part of "The H-P Way", the widely acclaimed management style of the Hewlett-Packard computer company (which also involved management by walking about – MBWA, see page 144). At every level within Hewlett-Packard, managers had to develop objectives and integrate them with those of other managers and of the company as a whole. This was done by producing written plans showing what people needed to achieve if they were to reach those objectives. The plans were then shared with others in the corporation and co-ordinated.

Bill Packard, one of the two founders of Hewlett-Packard, said of MBO:

> No operating policy has contributed more to Hewlett-Packard's success ... MBO ... is the antithesis of management by control. The latter refers to a tightly controlled system of management of the military type ... Management by

objectives, on the other hand, refers to a system in which overall objectives are clearly stated and agreed upon, and which gives people the flexibility to work toward those goals in ways they determine best for their own areas of responsibility.

Management by objectives is now largely ignored. Its once widely used abbreviation, MBO, has been taken over by the better known management buy-out, the purchasing of a company by its managers using debt to finance the deal.

Recommended reading

Drucker, P., *The Practice of Management*, Harper and Row, 1954

Koontz, H., O'Donnell, C. and Weihrich, H., *Essentials of Management*, McGraw Hill, 1982

Levinson, H., "Management by Whose Objectives?", *Harvard Business Review*, July-August 1970

Odiorne, G.S., *Management by Objectives: a System of Managerial Leadership*, Fearon Pitman, 1965

Odiorne, G.S., *MBO II: A System of Managerial Leadership for the 80s*, Fearon Pitman, 1979

Management by walking about

A phrase used to refer to a style of management commonly referred to as MBWA. This is variously lengthened to management by wandering about, or management by walking around. MBWA usually involves the following.

- Managers consistently reserving time to walk through their departments and/or to be available for impromptu discussions. (MBWA frequently goes together with an open-door management policy.)
- Individuals forming networks of acquaintances throughout their organisations.
- Lots of opportunities for chatting over coffee or lunch, or in the corridors.
- Managers getting away from their desks and starting to talk to individual employees. The idea is that they should learn about problems and concerns at first hand. At the same time they should teach employees new methods to manage particular problems. The communication goes both ways.

As W. Edwards Deming, an American who introduced the idea of quality management to the Japanese, put it:

> If you wait for people to come to you, you'll only get small problems. You must go and find them. The big problems are where people don't realise they have one in the first place.

The difficulty with MBWA is that (certainly at first) employees suspect it is an excuse for managers to spy and interfere unnecessarily. This suspicion usually falls away if the walkabouts occur regularly, and if everyone can see their benefits. MBWA has been found to be particularly helpful when an organisation is under exceptional stress; for instance, after a significant corporate reorganisation has been announced. It is no good practising MBWA for the first time on such an occasion, however. It has to have been a regular practice before the stress arises.

A brief history

In the late 1990s it did not seem extraordinary that managers should manage by walking about. But in the 1950s many white-collar managers turned their offices into ivory towers from which they rarely emerged. Edicts were sent out to a blue-collar workforce that they rarely met face-to-face. The outside world was filtered through to them via a secretary who, traditionally, sat like a guard dog in front of their (usually closed) office door.

Coming from this culture, MBWA was revolutionary. It was popularised by becoming an important part of "The H-P Way", the open style of management pioneered by the two founders of the Hewlett-Packard computer company, Bill Hewlett and Bill Packard. Many of the practices of The H-P Way became widely copied by corporations throughout the United States in the 1980s and early 1990s.

The idea received a further boost when Tom Peters (the guru of Excellence, see page 89) wrote in his second book (*A Passion for Excellence*) that he saw "managing by wandering about" as the basis of leadership and excellence. Peters called MBWA the "technology of the obvious". As leaders and managers wander about, he said that at least three things should be going on.

- They should be listening to what people are saying.
- They should be using the opportunity to transmit the company's values face to face.
- They should be prepared and able to give people on-the-spot help.

Recommended reading
Peters, T., and Austin, N., *A Passion for Excellence*, Collins, 1985

Mass customisation

Mass customisation refers to a production process that combines elements of mass production with the old-fashioned attributes of the craftsman. Products are tailored to meet a customer's individual needs. In mass customisation, no two items are the same.

Mass customisation uses some of the techniques of mass production; for example, its production process is based on a small number of platforms, core components that underlie the product. In the case of a watch, the internal mechanism is a platform to which can be added a wide variety of personalised options at later stages of production. Thus the purchaser of a Swatch watch has thousands of different options in terms of colour, straps, facia, and so on. Yet all are based on only a few time-keeping mechanisms. The same is increasingly true of cars. The Swatch car (which followed the same principles as the Swatch watch) is an obvious example. But even a traditional mass production manufacturer like BMW can now boast that no two of its new cars are identical.

Mass customisation is made possible by the use of information technology. Levi Strauss, which pioneered the idea in 1994 with its Original Spin jeans for women, measures customers in its stores and sends their measurements electronically to its factory. The customised jeans are then cut electronically and mailed to the customer.

The Internet has greatly increased the possibilities for mass customisation. Dell Computer company, for example, established its leadership of the PC market by allowing customers more or less to assemble their own PCs online. The company then put together the components as requested at the last minute before delivery. Ford also allows customers to build a vehicle from a palette of online options.

Companies that get into difficulties introducing mass customisation do so largely on two counts.

- They fail to define clearly the dimensions along which they are prepared to allow their customers to individualise their purchase. This leads to unnecessary cost and complexity. Dell Computer and the Swatch watch company do not offer consumers infinite choice. They are not trying to be all things to all customers. Consumers generally prefer to be told what their limits are, and then to be allowed free rein within them. Successful mass customisers first find out what limits their customers are happy to live within, and then they organise their operations accordingly. This contact with customers enables these companies to remain permanently in touch with fickle shifts in consumer tastes.

◪ They fail to shift their production satisfactorily from a system based on a series of tightly integrated processes, as demanded by mass production, to a system of loosely linked autonomous units that can be configured as and when the consumer wishes. As Joseph Pine, a respected writer on the subject, puts it: "Mass customisation organisations never know what customers will ask for next. All they can do is strive to be ever more prepared to meet the next request."

Another danger is that mass customisation becomes so popular that it detracts customers from more profitable sales opportunities. A company in California, for instance, offered booths in record shops where customers could put together cassette tapes from the recordings of a wide range of artists. It soon found that this service was such a hit that it was cannibalising sales of traditional cassettes and CDs.

A brief history
The idea of mass customisation grew in popularity in the 1980s and 1990s in response to the consumer's increasing willingness to pay for something that stood out as different from standard mass-produced goods and services.

Joseph Pine has pushed the idea a step further. In *Every Business a Stage* he proposes that we are on the threshold of what he calls "the experience economy", a new economic era in which businesses will have to orchestrate memorable events for their customers. It will not be enough merely to flog products and services, no matter how individualised they are. Examples of early movers into the experience economy include Starbucks coffee shops. It is the quality of the overall experience that enables the chain to charge premium prices for its products.

Recommended reading
Pine, B.J. II and Gilmore, J.H., "The Four Faces of Mass Customisation", *Harvard Business Review*, January-February 1997
Pine, B.J. II, *Mass Customisation: The New Frontier in Business Competition*, Harvard Business School Press, 1999
Pine, B.J. II and Gilmore, J.H., *Every Business a Stage*, Harvard Business School Press, 1999

Mass production

Mass production is a way of manufacturing things en masse (and for the masses), taking the initiative out of the hands of the consumer and putting it into the hands of the manufacturer. Before mass production methods were introduced, producers made things to order. They did not, by and large, manufacture things in the vague hope of selling them at some later date. They made things when they knew they had a customer.

In Elizabethan times, shops were not stuffed with goods waiting for buyers. They were full of craftsmen waiting to fulfil orders. With mass-production methods, manufacturers produce things in large quantities without having orders for them in advance. They worry about selling them later, the price they pay for enjoying economies of scale (see page 76) in the manufacturing process.

Mass production is based on the principles of specialisation and division of labour as first described by Adam Smith in the *Wealth of Nations* in 1776, and as first practised in places like Eli Whitney's gun factory in the 1790s. Mass-production methods use highly skilled labour to design products and set up production systems, and unskilled labour to produce standardised components and then to assemble them (with the help of specialised machinery). The early businesses using such methods were thus able to take workers directly out of agricultural labour on the land and on to the factory floor. No significant retraining was required.

The parts used in mass production are often manufactured elsewhere and then put together on a moving production facility known as an assembly line. The result is a standardised product made in a fairly small number of varieties, produced at low cost and of mediocre quality. The work is repetitive, and the workers are regarded as a variable cost to be taken on or laid off as demand dictates. In factories that are designed on the principles of mass production, stopping an assembly line to correct a problem at any one point stops work at all points. To reduce expensive stoppages of this sort, such factories generally hold large stocks of spares.

A brief history

The seminal event in the history of mass production was the appearance of the Model T car which, to quote the Ford Motor Company, "chugged into history on October 1st 1908". Henry Ford himself called it the "universal car", and it became so popular that, by the end of 1913, Ford was making half of all the cars produced in the United States.

To keep up with demand, says Ford's official record of events:

> [The company] initiated mass production in the factory. Mr
> Ford reasoned that with each worker remaining in one
> assigned place, with one specific task to do, the automobile
> would take shape more quickly as it moved from section to
> section and countless man-hours would be saved. To test the
> theory, a chassis was dragged by rope and windlass along
> the floor of the Highland Park, Michigan, plant in the
> summer of 1913. Modern mass production was born!
> Eventually, Model T's were rolling off the assembly lines at
> the rate of one every 10 seconds of each working day.

The moving assembly line was the start of an industrial revolution. In the 19 years that the Model T was in production, over 15m cars were produced and sold in the United States alone. Ford became an industrial complex that was the envy of every industrialist in the world.

In *Innovation in Marketing*, Theodore Levitt, a Harvard professor, gave an alternative view of the Ford saga.

> [Henry Ford's real genius] was marketing. We think he was
> able to cut his selling price and therefore sell millions of
> $500 cars because his invention of the assembly line had
> reduced the costs. Actually he invented the assembly line
> because he had concluded that at $500 he could sell
> millions of cars. Mass production was the result, not the
> cause of his low prices.

Not until the Japanese introduced techniques like just-in-time (see page 123) did manufacturing industry again experience anything like such a dramatic change. And not until the late 20th century did the development of the Internet threaten to bring about such radical change that the initiative in the buyer/seller relationship would shift back again, out of the hands of manufacturers and into the hands of the consumer.

Recommended reading

Ford, H., *My Life and Work*, 1923
Levitt, T., *Innovation in Marketing*, McGraw-Hill, 1962
Smith, A., *The Wealth of Nations*, 1776

Matrix management

Matrix management is a system for running companies that have both a diversity of products and a diversity of markets; that is, most businesses bigger than a family firm. In a matrix structure, the responsibility for the company's products goes up and down one dimension; responsibility for its markets goes up and down another. This leaves most managers with a dual reporting line: to the head of their product division on the one hand, and to the head of their geographical market on the other.

A brief history

Despite the potential confusion that this duality creates, matrix management was enormously popular in the 1970s and 1980s. Leading the way was a Dutch multinational electronics company, Philips, which first set up a matrix structure after the second world war. It had national organisations (NOS) and product divisions (PDS), and for a while they operated successfully as a network. The network was held together by a number of co-ordinating committees, which resolved any conflict between the two.

The crux came with the profit and loss account. Who was to be held accountable for it? At first, the answer was both the NOS and the PDS. But this was unsatisfactory, and the NOS eventually got the upper hand. Philips's PDS did not like it, and they fought back. By the 1990s, however, Philips was not doing so well, and its organisational structure was completely overhauled. A few powerful product divisions were given worldwide responsibility for the profit and loss account, and the national offices became subservient to them. This did not, however, mark the death of matrix management.

In an article in the *Harvard Business Review* in 1990, Christopher Bartlett and Sumantra Ghoshal suggested that the problem (especially for multinationals) was that:

> *Dual reporting led to conflict and confusion; the proliferation of channels created informational log-jams as a proliferation of committees and reports bogged down the organisation; and overlapping responsibilities produced turf battles and a loss of accountability. Separated by barriers of distance, language, time and culture, managers found it*

virtually impossible to clarify the confusion and resolve the conflicts.

The authors maintained that matrix management had been part of an attempt by companies to create complicated structures that matched their increasingly complicated strategies. But it focused only on the anatomy of the organisation. It ignored the physiology (the systems that allow information to flow in and around the organisation), and the psychology (the "shared norms, values and beliefs" of the organisation's managers). Organisations could implement matrix management successfully, Bartlett and Ghoshal claimed, if they started at the other end. Their first objective should be "to alter the organisational psychology ... only later do they consolidate and confirm their progress by realigning organisational anatomy through changes in the formal structure".

Nigel Nicholson of the London Business School says that the matrix structure is "one of the most difficult and least successful organisational forms". Evolutionists like him allege that matrix forms are inherently unstable because they have conflicting forces pulling towards too many different centres of gravity.

Matrix management still has its admirers, although most of them think that it works best in situations where there is a limited task involved and where everyone shares a strong sense of purpose. This includes situations like launching a new product or starting a new business, or something like putting on a Broadway show or getting a man to the moon.

Recommended reading

Bartlett, C. and Ghoshal, S., "Matrix Management: Not a Structure, A Frame of Mind", *Harvard Business Review*, July-August 1990
Nicholson, N., "How Hardwired is Human Behaviour?", *Harvard Business Review*, July-August 1998.

Mentoring

Mentoring is a relationship between two people in which one of them offers advice and guidance to help the other to develop in a particular area. This has occurred for centuries in the arts: musicians and painters have traditionally sat at the feet of a master, their mentor, to learn from him. Today, sports stars invariably have a trainer, an individual who looks after not only their physical fitness but also their mental preparedness for what it is that they want to do.

In the 1990s there was a sudden enthusiasm for developing this sort of relationship within the business environment. It reflected a number of things taking place at the time.

- A realisation that the pace of change was accelerating rapidly, and that in order to be successful businesses had to improve their understanding of its implications (see Change management, page 29). Mentoring (by an outsider) was seen as one way of helping managers to view the wider context of change in which their businesses were operating.
- A shift in emphasis within the business community back to the individual. Business was seen to have its stars, just like tennis or athletics, and these individuals needed mentors to help them prepare for their business tasks. It was not enough to go to conferences and seminars (which had previously been the main channel for development and learning). Managers needed to chew the cud with someone they could respect and trust. These individuals did not have to be brilliant managers themselves, any more than a tennis star's coach needs to be a brilliant tennis player. But they did have to have reached a certain level of knowledge and skill in order to have a proper appreciation of the technical and psychological issues facing the person for whom they were acting as mentor.
- The awareness (or, more correctly, the expression of an awareness) that it is lonely at the top. It became acceptable to admit that senior executives are, by force, cut off and restricted in whom they can talk to and in what they can say to other people within the same organisation. A mentor from outside can set problems in a wider context and chat about them in a disinterested, non-

confrontational way.

Managers can be mentored and mentors at the same time, in the same way that an athletics star can be a mentor for an up-and-coming young athlete, even while the older person is still competing in the sport (a role played by Lynford Christie in British sprinting, for example).

Mentoring does not just happen, however. It has to be formalised to a certain extent. A suitable mentor has to be found systematically, and meetings have to be arranged and held at regular intervals. But within these meetings there need be no agenda – just a mutual interest, good communication skills and some available spare time.

A brief history

Mentoring programmes are widespread in the United States, in both corporations and not-for-profit organisations. In the UK only a few companies, such as Lloyds TSB and British Gas, have made widespread use of them.

It is suggested that they are particularly helpful for managers who are sent on overseas postings. A knowledgeable mentor can help someone to settle into a new culture and to overcome the difficulties that so frequently cause overseas postings to end in early failure.

Recommended reading

Lewis, G., *The Mentoring Manager*, Pitman, 1996

Mission statement

A mission statement is an organisation's vision (see page 238) translated into written form. It makes concrete (for all to see and read) the leaders' view of the direction and purpose of the organisation. For many corporate leaders it is a vital element in any attempt to motivate employees and to give them a sense of priorities. Mission statements generally address a number of important questions.

- What is the purpose of the organisation?
- What is unique about the organisation?
- What are its principal products and markets?
- What are its values?
- Where is it hoping to be in five or ten years' time?

The challenge is to distil all this into a short, pithy paragraph that will be memorable to all those with an interest in the company, and that will motivate them in the required direction at all moments of their working life.

It is easy for a mission statement to become a bland idealistic blur, as in this thinly disguised (real) example: "The mission of X is to maximise the company value by providing total quality services, empowering customer-oriented employees and growing through expansion, acquisition and new technology." Such jargon is not likely to fire an imagination struggling to establish the company's services in an entirely new market.

Many companies buttress their mission statements with a catchy slogan, something which does not aspire to answer the questions listed above but which acts as a quick and easy guide to what the company is really about. The best of these can be taken at several different levels and suit many purposes; for example, Harley-Davidson's "It's not the destination, it's the journey"; Nike's "Just do it"; and IBM's "Solutions for a small planet".

Three main benefits are attributed to mission statements.

- They can help companies to focus their strategy by defining some boundaries within which to operate. Federal Express, for example, says it is "dedicated to maximising financial returns by providing totally reliable, competitively superior, global air-ground transportation of high priority goods and documents that require rapid, time-certain delivery". It is not, therefore, going to enter the business of bulk shipping oil products or semiconductors.

◼ They can define the dimensions along which an organisation's performance is to be measured and judged. The most common candidate (not surprisingly) is profit. Du Pont, for example, says that it considers itself successful "only if we return to our shareholders a long-term financial reward comparable to the better performing large industrial companies". Corporations often acknowledge their responsibility to other stakeholders as well, mentioning their attitude to employees ("to treat them with respect, promote teamwork, and encourage personal freedom and growth" – Dow Chemical), to customers ("to continually exceed our customers' increasing expectations" – Johnson Controls) and to society in general ("to help people live longer and fuller lives" – Pharmacia & Upjohn).

◼ They can suggest standards for individual ethical behaviour (see Ethical business, page 86). For example, the Body Shop in the UK has what it calls "Our reasons for being". Among them are: "To passionately campaign for the protection of the environment, human and civil rights, and against animal testing within the cosmetics and toiletries industries."

A brief history

A number of large, successful companies have laid great store by their mission statements. Johnson & Johnson, for example, one of the most admired companies in the United States, has the J&J Credo. It was written in 1943 by Robert W. Johnson Jr when he succeeded his father as chairman of what was then still essentially a family firm. The J&J Credo sets priorities by stating that J&J's first responsibility is to its customers. Its second responsibility is to its employees, its third to its management, its fourth to the community, and its fifth and last is to its shareholders.

At IBM, Thomas J. Watson Jr wrote in his 1963 book about the firm which his father founded that its three fundamental values were:

◼ a respect for the individual;
◼ unparalleled customer service; and
◼ the pursuit of superiority in all that the company undertakes.

Steve Jobs's mission statement for Apple in 1980 was: "To make a contribution to the world by making tools for the mind that advance humankind".

The idea of mission statements got a big boost (and the name) from the wide publicity given to that of the NASA moon mission articulated by President Kennedy in 1961: "Achieving the goal, before this decade is out, of landing a man on the moon and returning him safely to earth." This mission was achieved, just in time, in July 1969.

James Collins and Jerry Porras, authors of *Built to Last: Successful Habits of Visionary Companies*, say that there are four approaches to setting a mission.

1 Targeting. This can be precise, as was NASA's, and as was that of the Wal-Mart supermarket chain, which set itself a target in 1976 of being a $1 billion company within four years – which it achieved. Or it can be less precise; for example, Merck's 1979 target of becoming "the pre-eminent drug-maker worldwide in the 1980s".

2 Common enemy. This is perhaps most famously embodied in Honda's three-word mission statement – "*Yamaha wo tsubusu*" ("We will crush Yamaha") – proving that Japanese firms are as fiercely competitive among themselves as they are abroad. Nike, a sports-shoe manufacturer, also thrived on a mission to defeat the enemy, first adidas, then Reebok.

3 Role model. This is less common than the first two and crops up in the form of: "To be the IBM of the real-estate business" or "To be the Rolls-Royce of the shoe industry".

4 Internal transformation. This is often used by old organisations in need of a shake-up. Procter & Gamble, for instance, sought at one time to provide its workers with steady employment following a period when it had become known for its rapid hire-and-fire policies.

Recommended reading

Collins, J. and Porras, J., *Built to Last: Successful Habits of Visionary Companies*, HarperBusiness, 1994

Collins, J. and Porras, J., "Organisational Vision and Visionary Organisations", *California Management Review*, 1997

Haschak, P., *Corporate Statements, the official missions, goals, principles and philosophies of over 900 companies*, McFarland & Co, 1998

Niche market

A niche market is a group of potential customers who share common characteristics that make them receptive to a particular product or service. This characteristic may be no more complicated than the fact that they have run out of socks without holes (the group to which the British niche retailer Sock Shop was appealing).

Launching a product into a niche market is far cheaper than launching a mass-market product. The potential customers are easier to identify and to target. Niche markets often develop from mass markets (the market for invalid cars, for example, or for left-handed oven gloves), and mass-market manufacturers sometimes choose to launch niche products as well. Chrysler, for instance, manufactures the Dodge Viper, a niche vehicle that sells in extremely limited quantities to hard-core motor enthusiasts. Ford produces the Aston Martin, and Fiat the Ferrari.

Conversely, what are expected to be niche markets sometimes develop into mass markets. When Apple came up with the PC in the early 1980s, for instance, it did not expect it to become a mass-market product. Yet it did, and out of that mass market there ultimately emerged some niches, such as the educational PC market.

The trouble with niche markets that do not develop into mass markets is that they soon reach their maximum size. A niche, which can be so helpful in getting a product off the ground, can soon become a straitjacket. Manufacturers have to find another niche product, or another market in which to sell their existing product. Specialist food suppliers in Scotland, for instance, soon need to spread south to England, and then across the Channel to the rest of Europe. Or they need to add oatcakes to their range of smoked salmon and cock a'leekie soup.

The Internet has features that make it ideal for niche marketing. Through its mailing lists and newsgroups it gathers electronically in one spot of cyberspace precisely those groups of customers with similar interests that are a niche marketer's dream. Mailing lists and newsgroups focus on specific topics. In each discussion group there can be as many as 10,000 regular readers with a special interest in that topic. There are discussion groups on doll collecting, car racing, cycling in the Himalayas – almost anything you care to mention.

A brief history

Some have seen niche marketing as a phase in a 20th-century journey from mass marketing to one-to-one marketing. Nowhere has this journey been better described than in *MaxiMarketing* by Stan Rapp and Tom Collins:

> *The 50s and 60s were the heyday of mass marketing. There was one kind of Coca-Cola soft drink for the thirsty ... one kind of Holiday Inn motel for the traveller. The 70s became a decade of segmentation and line extension. It was followed in the early 80s by intensified niche marketing that sliced markets into smaller and smaller groups of consumers ... by the mid-80s Robitussin was offering four kinds of medicine for four kinds of cough ... from mass marketing to segmented marketing to niche marketing to tomorrow's world of one-to-one marketing – the transformation will be complete by the end of the 80s.*

That was written in 1987, and the authors' crystal ball got a bit fuzzy at the end. Ten years later than they forecast, by the end of the 1990s, the Internet promised to bring about the one-to-one marketing of goods and services – tailored for a single individual rather than a class of individuals – that they had foreseen as the next step after niche marketing.

Recommended reading

Linnerman, R.E. and Stanton, J.L., *Making Niche Marketing Work – How to Grow Bigger by Acting Smaller*, McGraw Hill, 1991

Rapp, S. and Collins, T., *MaxiMarketing*, McGraw-Hill, 1987

Open-book management

The still unconventional idea that firms are most effective if their accounts are left open for their employees to see as and when they wish, at the same time as these employees are taught to understand the big financial picture. Traditionally, only a handful of senior executives are made to feel responsible for whether a business makes money or not. Open-book management attempts to extend this feeling of responsibility to everybody in the organisation.

It is described by John Case, the man who claims to have invented the expression, as the idea "that companies do better when employees care not just about quality, efficiency or any other single performance variable, but about the same thing that senior managers are supposed to care about: the success of the business". It broadens the concept of P&L responsibility (the responsibility for the profit and loss account of a business unit that is generally given as a reward to rising managers) to everyone in the organisation. With open-book management everyone is made to feel they have a certain amount of P&L responsibility.

Open-book management is backed by the same sort of logic that persuades parents to leave household bills lying around in sight of their teenage children, in the (frequently vain) hope that the children will make different economic choices if they can see that their telephone bills are much the same as the price of a Caribbean vacation. A corporation's gain from open-book management comes from the extra motivation that employees may get from knowing its true situation, and from feeling that they are trusted not to abuse that information. The danger is that proprietary information will be spread to rivals, and that if business is bad, employees will be damagingly demotivated. Moreover, not every employee wants details of their salary to be bandied about.

The issue is sometimes seen in terms of the long-running management debate about Theories X and Y (see page 223). Are employees to be trusted with corporate financial information, or are they to be treated as little more than wage slaves? A chief executive once remarked that "anyone in charge of an organisation with more than two people is running a clinic". Open-book management can turn the clinic into bedlam.

A brief history
Although John Case, a journalist with *Inc.* magazine, claims credit for the

invention of the expression, the idea of open-book management was pioneered by a company called Springfield ReManufacturing Corporation. It opened its books to its employees in 1983, and a book called *The Great Game of Business*, written by the company's president, Jack Stack, in 1992, documented the company's experience. Every other Wednesday, 35–40 Springfield employees would sit around a U-shaped table and receive a financial presentation from the company's finance director. Departments would also report their results to the meeting. The exercise is said to have made the company's employees act more like business people and less like hired hands.

Several companies have used open-book management as part of an attempt to generate intrapreneurship (see page 120), a sense of entrepreneurship among full-time employees. They have also used it in line with compensation schemes that are related to the business's performance. In one company, the boss quizzed employees on the company's profit and loss account and rewarded correct answers with $50 bonuses handed over on the spot.

R.R. Donnelley, the world's largest printing firm, adopted open-book management and found that it failed to live up to expectations. However, Case claims to have found over 100 other US-based companies that have raised profits by opening up their books in one form or another.

He sees open-book management as providing the solution to a problem raised by the idea of empowerment (see page 80) – namely that empowered employees will strive only to better their own individual performance, or (at best) that of their team, rather than that of the company overall. Only if they are made to feel part of a business that is competing in a market place (with all that this entails) will they be motivated to work for the general good of the organisation. But even Case says that it takes up to four years to make the culture change that is necessary for open-book management to work.

Recommended reading

Case, J., *Open-book management: the coming business revolution*, HarperBusiness, 1995

Case, J., "Opening the Books (open-book management)", *Harvard Business Review*, March-April 1997

Davis, T.R.V., "Open-book management: its promise and pitfalls", *Organizational Dynamics*, Winter 1997

Kroll, K.M., "By the Books (open-book management)", *Industry Week*, July 1997

Operational research

According to the Operational Research Society:

> *Operational Research* (OR), *also known as Operations Research or Management Science* (OR/MS), *looks at an organisation's operations and uses mathematical or computer models, or other analytical approaches, to find better ways of doing them.*

Operational research is to managers what econometrics is to economists. The term "operational research" is generally used in the UK; the United States favours "operations research" or "management science".

At the heart of OR is the use of computer modelling and the simulation of business processes as a means of coming up with improvements in the way that things are done within a corporation. The tasks that OR examines are complex and involve many variables. They include things like designing an optimal telecommunications network in a situation where future demand is uncertain, or automating a paper-based bank clearing system.

Information technology is central to the skill of an operational researcher. But OR also draws on mathematics, engineering, physics and economics. Operational researchers were "rocket scientists" before that term was invented.

A brief history

Operational research acted as an intellectual bridge between the early mechanism of Frederick Taylor's scientific management (see page 193) and of Frank Gilbreth's time and motion studies, and the later mechanism of just-in-time (see page 123) and of quality management systems. (Gilbreth pioneered the use of cameras to help find the best way to carry out the different operations involved in a particular manufacturing process.)

The heyday of OR was in the 1950s and 1960s when, as Russell Ackoff, an OR academic, once put it, "use of quantitative methods became an 'idea in good currency'". By the 1990s, though, Ackoff found that OR had been pushed into "the bowels of the organisation not the head. When it could no longer be pushed down, it was pushed out". This, he believed, was because OR had been "equated by managers to mathematical masturbation and to the absence of any substantive knowledge or understanding of organisations, institutions or their management". Ackoff also claimed that there was a more fundamental flaw to OR. It is, he said, designed to "prepare perfectly for an imperfectly predicted future", and it "helps us little and may harm us much".

Igor Ansoff, author of the classic *Corporate Strategy* (see Strategic planning, page 206), was heavily influenced by the time he spent working on sophisticated operational research for the Rand Foundation in the early 1950s. Among other things, he analysed the extent of the exposure of NATO air forces to enemy attack.

Operational research helps to explain why so many engineers have been successful management thinkers, including Frederick Taylor, W. Edwards Deming (the founder of the quality movement), Henry Mintzberg, Bruce Henderson (the founder of the Boston Consulting Group) and Ansoff himself. The skills of the engineer in structuring a physical entity are much the same as those required by the operational researcher in designing an ideal operation. Trained engineers like Ansoff often came into general management via operational research.

Recommended reading
Ackoff, R.L., *Redesigning the Future*, John Wiley, 1974
Beer, S., *The Meaning of Operational Research and Management Cybernetics*, John Wiley, 1994
Taha, H.A., *Operations Research: an Introduction*, Macmillan, 1971
Operational Research Quarterly
Journal of the Operational Research Society

Outsourcing

Outsourcing is a term used to describe almost any corporate activity that is managed by an outside vendor: from the running of the company's cafeteria to the provision of courier services. It is most commonly used, however, to apply to the transfer of the management of an organisation's computer facilities to an outside agent. This transfer of management responsibility is frequently accompanied by a transfer (from the buyer of the outsourcing service to the vendor) of the specialist staff who are carrying out the activity.

Outsourcing has three main advantages.

- The first comes from the way in which greater economies of scale (see page 76) can be gained by a third party that is able to pool the activity of a large number of firms. It is thus frequently cheaper for a firm to outsource specialised activities (where it cannot hope to gain economies of scale on its own) than it is to carry them out itself.
- The second comes from the ability of a specialist outsourcing firm to keep abreast of the latest developments in its field. This has been a particularly significant factor in the area of information technology, where technological change has been so rapid that many companies' in-house capabilities have been insufficient to keep up with it.
- The third comes from the way that it enables small firms to do things for which they could not possibly justify hiring employees full-time, such as accounting, distribution and marketing.

The most commonly cited disadvantage of outsourcing is the loss of control involved in derogating responsibility for particular processes to others. In the command-and-control type of organisational model this is problematic. In such a model, a firm that does not own all the processes involved in manufacturing its products or services is not thought to be in proper control of its own destiny, any more than is an army made up of different bands of mercenaries.

A brief history

Outsourcing is not a new phenomenon. Companies have outsourced their advertising, for instance, for almost as long as advertising has been in existence (and J. Walter Thompson has been in business since the 1880s). Financial services such as factoring and leasing, the outsourcing respectively of the accounts receivable function and of capital funding, have also been available from outside providers for many years.

Outsourcing has been increasing since the second world war, and especially rapidly in the 1990s. According to one estimate, in 1946 only 20% of a typical American manufacturing company's value-added in production and operations came from outside sources; 50 years later the proportion had tripled to 60%.

Much of the rapid increase in the 1990s came from the outsourcing of IT functions. This was bolstered later by the outsourcing of other functions (such as logistics) that were in areas that themselves had a high degree of IT content. Banks, for instance, began to outsource the IT-intensive processing of financial instruments such as loans or mortgage-backed securities. The savings from such moves could be dramatic. By deciding to outsource the origination, packaging and servicing of all its personal loans, both old and new, one British bank cut the average cost of processing them by over 75%.

Outsourcing's attractions have been reinforced by the fact that in many industries the biggest outsourcers were also the most profitable firms. In the car industry in the 1990s, for example, firms with the biggest profit per car, such as Toyota, Honda and Chrysler, were also the biggest outsourcers (sourcing around 70% to various suppliers). Those that outsourced the least (General Motors, for example, which outsourced only 30% of its value added) were the least profitable.

The nature of outsourcing contracts has changed over time. What started off as a straightforward arm's-length agreement between a buyer and a supplier soon moved on to become structured more like a partnership. In this, not only is any increase in the clients' volume of business reflected in the outsourcer's scale of charges, but both parties in some way share the risks and rewards of the outsourced activity.

An example is the 1997 deal between IBM and a chemicals company, Monsanto. In the first part of the agreement, Monsanto outsourced much of its IT operations to IBM for ten years. In the second part, the two firms agreed to set up the IBM/Monsanto Solution Center, a unit that was to offer services to other companies (third parties) trying to implement enterprise resource planning systems (ERP; see page 82). In a third stage of the deal, the two firms planned to collaborate on genomics research.

Relationships like this vary over time and require firms to learn how to work together in entirely new ways. In the early 1990s, in a groundbreaking five-year outsourcing agreement with BP, Andersen Consulting took over responsibility for running the day-to-day operation of BP's accounting systems. BP retained control of accounting policy and the interpretation of data for business decision-making. In return, Andersen Consulting guaranteed BP that it would reduce the cost of running the service by 20%; in practice, costs were cut by some 40%.

Some firms have been so taken with the idea of outsourcing that they have left themselves with little to do in their own name. An American company called Monorail Computers, for instance, outsources the manufacture of its computers as well as the ordering, delivery and the accounts receivable. Only the design, the company's core competence (see page 40), is handled in-house.

The Pareto Principle (the 80/20 principle)

Vilfredo Pareto was a 19th-century professor of political economy at the University of Lausanne who had a moment of brilliance. In it, he recognised that in many markets around the world the majority of the activity was accounted for by a minority of the operators. This has come to be known as the 80/20 principle: 80% of the activity comes from 20% of the operators.

Pareto himself was most interested in applying his principle to the wealth of nations, the bulk of which (then as now) was in the hands of a small minority of the population. He discovered that the distribution of income in different countries was remarkably similar; for example, the top 20% of any population always accounted for more or less the same percentage of total income.

As an Italian born in Paris who was working in Switzerland, Pareto had an insight into several national income distributions. From his findings he deduced that there was a law governing the distribution, and from this he concluded that policies to redistribute incomes would not work. The only way to increase the income of the poor, he maintained, was to increase the size of the cake; that is, to increase production (GDP). This has been the view of many politicians since.

Pareto's law, however, has been discredited. Income distributions do shift over time, if not sufficiently dramatically to please everybody. Nevertheless, his idea has been widely influential in management thinking about markets.

A brief history

Robert Townsend's view of Pareto's Principle, expounded in his comic classic *Up the Organisation*, was that "20% of any group of salesmen will always produce 90% of the sales" – not an 80/20 rule but a 90/20 rule. The principle has been applied to a wide variety of markets, from fishing (where 20% of the fishermen catch 80% of the fish) to advertising (where 20% of any advertising campaign produces 80% of the response, or something of that order) to publishing (where 20% of the books produce 80% of the profits).

The Boston Consulting Group says that the principle also applies in mergers and acquisitions. In the post-merger phase, many new projects have to be implemented if the full benefits of a merger are to be achieved.

BCG has found that 65% of these benefits come from 35% of the projects – a 65/35 rule.

Recommended reading

Pareto, V., *Cours d'économie politique*, 1897
Townsend, R., *Up the Organisation*, Michael Joseph, 1970

Performance-related pay

Any system that relates the rewards of an individual employee to the performance of the organisation that they work for is called performance-related pay, commonly referred to as PRP. Such systems are designed to motivate employees and to align their effort more closely with the aims of the organisation. The pay is often financial, but it can also be non-financial, anything from $10 Wal-Mart vouchers to transatlantic flights on Concorde. Payments under such schemes are usually made separately from regular salary payments. In this way the recipient appreciates that they are variable, separate and not guaranteed.

Sometimes the rise in an employee's annual basic salary is also performance related. This can be helpful in retaining employees who are at the top end of the pay scale according to their job ranking, but whose performance is still outstanding. Such employees are more numerous in the flatter organisations of today, where the opportunities for promotion to a higher rank are far fewer than they were in the multi-layered organisations of earlier years.

PRP schemes are most commonly used for managers in private-sector organisations. Technical, clerical and manual employees more rarely take part, even though (ironically) their performance can be more easily measured. Such schemes are generally self-funding; the improvement in performance more than pays for the rewards.

The advantages claimed for properly designed schemes are that they motivate people (via the financial reward and the recognition this gives to their achievement) and reward them more fairly. For the motivation to be maximised, individual employees must be able to see clearly the relationship between their performance and the rewards that they receive.

Critics argue that pay is not a major motivator in the workplace. They quote Fred Herzberg's view that the job itself is the source of true motivation, backing up their claim with studies such as the one where staff cited pay as fifth on their list of top ten motivators.

PRP schemes have a number of other drawbacks. It is often difficult to design an objective and fair measure of performance that does not emphasise the individual's effort at the expense of that of the team. It can also be difficult to base the rewards on the right time frame. If they are too short-term, they may not be in the best interests of the organisation as a whole; if they are too long-term, they may not be sufficiently motivating to the participants. Poorly designed PRP schemes can interfere with other programmes for improvement. One company, for instance, found that its attempts to introduce a just-in-time (see page 123) system were hindered by the reluctance of staff to undertake the necessary training. The training interfered with their productivity in the short term, and hence with their take-home pay.

A brief history

PRP schemes became increasingly popular in the 1980s and 1990s. One study found that in 1989 44% of American companies had PRP plans in place for employees other than senior management. By 1991 the figure had increased to 51%. A 1998 survey by the UK's Institute of Personnel and Development found that some 40% of a sample of British companies had PRP systems in operation at the time.

In their 1982 book *In Search of Excellence*, Tom Peters and Robert Waterman mentioned the great variety of non-monetary incentives used by the excellent companies that they studied. They said that excellent companies actively look for excuses to hand out rewards. At Hewlett-Packard, for instance, they came across members of the marketing team who would anonymously send 1lb bags of pistachio nuts to salesmen who sold a new machine.

Share-option schemes, which were regularly offered as part of performance-related pay in the late 1980s and early 1990s, gave the system a bad name. They succeeded in turning a few senior managers into multimillionaires, as much because of the general bullishness of the stockmarket as of the performance of the managers or of their business. They gave nothing to the many colleagues who had helped to hike up the share price. In many cases, such schemes demotivated more than they motivated.

By 1999 *The Economist* was writing that employers were looking for new ways to use pay as a motivator. "Instead of performance-related pay – too formulaic – the new mantra is 'variable pay': bonuses linked to the performance of the individual, the team or the company."

Recommended reading

Armstrong, M. and Baron, A., *Performance Management*, Institute of Personnel and Development, London, 1998

Greenhill, R.T., *Performance Related Pay: the Complete Guide*, Director Books, 1988

Herzberg, F., "One More Time: How do you Motivate your Employees?", *Harvard Business Review*, January-February 1968

Levinson, H., "Appraisal of What Performance?", *Harvard Business Review*, July-August 1976

Rappaport, A., "New Thinking on How to Link Executive Pay with Performance", *Harvard Business Review*, March-April 1999

The Peter Principle

The principle is encapsulated in the phrase, "In a hierarchy, every employee tends to rise to his level of incompetence". This phrase first appeared on the cover of a book, *The Peter Principle*, written by Laurence J. Peter and Raymond Hull and published in 1969. Written in a mock 19th-century style and illustrated with 19th-century engravings from *Punch*, a British humorous magazine, the book was an instant hit. Peter's Corollary stated: "In time, every post tends to be occupied by an employee who is incompetent to carry out its duties" or "the cream rises until it sours". As one reviewer wrote at the time: "There is a chilling touch of truth behind the whole thing."

Although Peter applied the principle mostly to the educational world with which he was familiar, it was not long before industrial hierarchies realised that it applied just as well to many of them. The tendency to over-promote people permeates every level of an organisation – from the marketing assistant who will never have what it takes to be a marketing manager to the outstanding finance director who is promoted to be CEO. Taken to extremes, it is a deeply depressing idea. It means that all employees, however efficient, are merely in transit, en route to a desk where they will be useless.

Peter's (tongue-in-cheek) solution to this "philosophy of despair" was to recommend "creative incompetence". Anyone who is in a job that they enjoy can avoid that ultimate promotion by creating "the impression that you have already reached your level of incompetence. Creative incompetence will achieve the best results if you choose an area of incompetence which does not directly hinder you in carrying out the main duties of your present position."

Peter and Hull suggested tactics such as:

- occasionally parking your car in the space reserved for the company president;
- arranging to receive a fake threatening phone call in the office and then pleading, within earshot of as many people as possible, "Don't tell my wife. If she finds out, this will kill her".

The book was written at a time when bureaucracy, and the mental attitudes that went with it, were far more pervasive than at the end of the

20th century. With the subsequent delayering (see page 62) of the hierarchies of many organisations, and with the growth in the number of people working completely outside hierarchies, much of the incompetence that Peter identified disappeared.

In parallel, so did much of the force of his principle. For one thing, it became much easier for people to move (and to be moved) from those stultifying final positions. Furthermore, it was no longer assumed that managers would be promoted, almost automatically, after a certain number of years. This did not, however, stop the phrase from becoming part of the English language.

A brief history

Peter's book came out of the blue. Hull was an unknown Canadian journalist and Peter himself was a Canadian teacher who had also been a counsellor, school psychologist, prison instructor and consultant. *The Peter Principle* sold over 1m copies, a remarkable feat for a book of its type at the time, and it spent no less than 33 weeks in the American bestsellers' list.

Recommended reading

Peter, L.J. and Hull, R., *The Peter Principle*, William Morrow, 1969

Planned obsolescence

Planned obsolescence is a business strategy in which the obsolescence (the process of becoming obsolete – that is, unfashionable or no longer usable) of a product is planned and built into it from its conception. This is done so that in future the consumer feels the need to purchase the new products and services that the manufacturer brings out as replacements for the old ones.

Consumers sometimes see planned obsolescence as a sinister plot by manufacturers to fleece them. But Philip Kotler, a marketing guru, says: "Much so-called planned obsolescence is the working of the competitive and technological forces in a free society – forces that lead to ever-improving goods and services."

A classic case of planned obsolescence was the nylon stocking. The inevitable "laddering" of stockings made consumers buy new ones and for years discouraged manufacturers from looking for a fibre that did not have this quality. The garment industry in general has built-in obsolescence because of the influence of fashion. Last year's skirts, for example, are rendered obsolete by this year's new models.

The strategy of planned obsolescence is common in the computer industry. New software is often carefully designed to reduce the value to consumers of the previous version. This is achieved by making programs upwardly compatible only; in other words, the new versions can read all the files of the old versions, but not the other way round. Someone holding the old version can communicate only with others using the old version. It is as if every generation of children came into the world speaking a completely different language from their parents, and while they could understand their parents' language, their parents could not understand theirs.

The production processes required for such a strategy to be successful are well illustrated by Intel. This American semiconductor firm is working on the production of the next generation of PC chips before it has begun to market the last one.

A strategy of planned obsolescence can backfire. If a manufacturer produces new products to replace old ones too often, consumer resistance can set in. This has occurred at times in the computer industry when consumers have been unconvinced that a new wave of replacement products is giving sufficient extra value for it to be worth their while to make the switch.

A brief history

As the life cycle of products increased towards the end of the century – largely because of their greater technical excellence – firms found that they needed to plan those products' obsolescence more carefully. Take, for instance, the example of the motor car. Its greater durability made consumers reluctant to exchange their models as frequently as they used to. As the useful life of the car was extended, manufacturers were forced to focus on shortening the car's fashionable life. By adding styling and cosmetic changes to their vehicles, they subtly attempted to make their older models look out-of-date, and thus to persuade consumers to trade them in for new ones.

Planned obsolescence is obviously not a strategy for the luxury car market. Marques such as Rolls-Royce rely on propagating the idea that they may (like antiques) one day be worth more than the price that was paid for them. They are not (yet) being manufactured with the idea that they should be replaced in three years' time.

Portfolio working

Portfolio working is a vision of the way that people will work in the future. It was clearly expounded by Charles Handy in his book *The Empty Raincoat*. He wrote:

> Going portfolio means exchanging full-time employment for independence. The portfolio is a collection of different bits and pieces of work for different clients. The word "job" now means a client ... I told my children when they were leaving education that they would be well advised to look for customers not bosses ... They have "gone portfolio" out of choice, for a time. Others are forced into it, when they get pushed outside by their organisation. If they are lucky, their old organisation will be the first client in their new portfolio. The important difference is that the price-tag now goes on their produce, not their time.

In her book, *Portfolio Working*, Joanna Grigg defines it as having "a group or cluster of different employers, or a job and a business, or whatever combination comes together best for us".

This is not a new way of working. It is based on the model of the self-employed professional – the individual accountant, lawyer or portrait photographer – who work for themselves, selling their skills to a number of clients. The cost of their work is not just a function of time. It is a function of the time plus, as the artist Whistler once famously put, "a lifetime of experience".

The life of a portfolio worker needs to be managed in a different way from that of a full-time employee. Portfolio workers are never unemployed. Like actors, they may be resting. But at that time they need to be marketing themselves, or they need to have a good agent doing it for them. Handy believes that the age of the portfolio worker will mark the return of the professional agent. A good agent, he says, will "help to organise your life so that there is some order in the necessary chaos of the independent's schedule".

Portfolio workers do not have a lot of the things that full-time employees take for granted, ranging from secretarial assistance to office parties. They also need to acquire a far wider range of skills, such as computer skills, marketing, accounting and filling in tax returns. They can learn a lot from the way in which professional service firms manage themselves. For example, such firms rely heavily on the apprenticeship system. Young "craftsmen" learn their business by working at the feet of a master. They earn very little, but both sides benefit.

Moreover, unlike full-time employees, portfolio workers cannot hope to find confirmation of a job well done (a vital part of any worker's motivation) from within their own organisation. They have to find it outside, primarily from their clients. This, it can be argued, makes them intensely customer-centric, something that should serve them well in the 21st century.

A brief history

Portfolio working has evolved from a growing belief that guarantees of permanent full-time employment cannot continue to exist for much longer. Downsizing (see page 71) and delayering (see page 62) shed many skilled workers in the late 1980s and 1990s, and they had no option but to become portfolio workers. The privatisation of state enterprises has also had an impact. These were often staffed by people who expected to be there for life. In many cases, the first thing that private-sector management did was to get rid of them.

Even government departments and universities (with their antiquated system of tenure, or lifetime job security) are realising that giving people jobs for life does not necessarily benefit their organisation. For a start, they now see that they can outsource (see page 163) a lot of the work that has traditionally been done by full-time permanent staff.

There has been demand-pull as well as supply-push operating in the market for portfolio workers. Many young people prefer to work in this way. With fewer worries about financial security, they see it as freeing them from the drudgery of the job-for-life that was frequently their parents' main ambition. They see portfolio working as a way of gaining freedom to plan their days, and as a chance to have a far more varied workload than the full-time employee.

Recommended reading

Grigg, J., *Portfolio Working*, Kogan Page, 1997
Handy, C., *The Empty Raincoat*, Hutchinson, 1994
Maister, D., *Managing the Professional Service Firm*, The Free Press, 1993

Post-merger integration

Post-merger integration (PMI) became a popular management issue in the 1990s as it was increasingly acknowledged that signing off on mergers and acquisitions (M&A) was easy. Just about anybody seemed able to do it. Making them work was the difficult part. What does it take to make a merger work?

Two reasons for the acknowledged high failure rate of mergers and acquisitions are:

- Giving too much attention to financial and strategic aspects during the negotiation of the deal. All eyes are focused on striking the right price (whatever it is). Instead, they should be be focused on making whatever price is paid worth it, by a subsequent successful integration of the two businesses.
- Underestimating the cultural differences between the two organisations. These can be particularly significant in deals that cross borders. An Anglo-French merger between packaging companies Metal Box and Carnaud, for instance, was notorious for the refusal of managers from different cultures to work with each other. It has sometimes been said that cross-border deals work well in the airline industry because people have gone into that particular business in order to meet and understand people from other cultures. The same cannot be said of people who go into packaging.

A survey by the Boston Consulting Group (BCG) of what its clients believe is important for successful mergers put "successful integration" at the top of the list, alongside "strategic fit". These two came well ahead of "choosing the best acquisition candidate", "paying the lowest price" and "structuring the best finance".

BCG says that the skills of PMI can be learned. The more that companies do it, the better they become at it. BCG says there are six essential lessons.

1 Clearly define the vision behind the deal, and then explain the strategy.
2 Manage the integration as a discrete process separate from the organisation's usual business.

3 Set up special integration teams with explicit tasks and schedules.
4 Give explicit targets for the benefits that are to come from the integration.
5 Build up effective human-resources processes as quickly as possible.
6 Design a programme to communicate the aims and progress of the integration, and then be quite explicit about it.

A brief history

Mergers and acquisitions have had a mixed track record over the years. Leon Cooperman, a senior executive at Goldman Sachs, a big investment banking adviser on M&A, when asked to name one big merger that had lived up to expectations, said: "I'm sure that there are success stories out there. But at this moment I draw a blank."

Michael Porter, who looked closely at the activities of 33 large American companies between 1950 and 1986, found that 55% of their acquisitions were later divested. Of their forays into unrelated industries (the fashion at the time was for conglomerates), 74% were later divested.

One of the most successful cross-border mergers in recent years was that between two engineering companies, Swedish Asea and Swiss Brown Boveri. It made a star of the chief executive of the merged company, Percy Barnevik. Asea-Brown Boveri (ABB) has a *Book of Values* in which it sets out basic guidelines for behaviour. In it, it says: "The true merger process does not come automatically or naturally. It is unnatural and takes management determination."

Process improvement

The terms process improvement, process excellence and process innovation all come from the work of Michael Hammer, the architect of re-engineering (see page 186). Re-engineering turned the spotlight on business processes. Indeed, it was often referred to as business process re-engineering (BPR). It often led firms to find ways of looking at processes in isolation, out of the context of re-engineering, and at ways in which those processes could be improved.

According to Andersen Consulting, a process is "a group of interrelated activities that together create value for the customer". It is something above and beyond the traditional functional division of corporate activities. A function, by itself, does not produce outcomes that are of value to customers. Accounting is a function, but it does not add value in its own right. It does so only when added to the production and selling that it is taking account of.

This distinction is crucial. Functions focus on completing tasks, but processes focus on delivering outcomes. Processes cut across functional departments, such as marketing, manufacturing and accounting. A company with a process mindset seeks to integrate groups of tasks, "unlike functional organisations that fragment work into ever smaller and simpler tasks".

Andersen Consulting has gone on to identify a number of dimensions along which change in processes can occur. Conveniently, they all begin with the letter R. The activities that make up a process can be:

- reconfigured;
- reordered;
- reallocated (to another manager);
- relocated (to another place); or
- reduced (to another size).

A superior process, says Andersen, has seven basic features.

1 It maximises value and eliminates waste. Robert Eaton, when chairman of Chrysler Corporation, said: "There is a definition that I like: Waste is anything that the customer won't pay for ... If you look at waste from that perspective, you find that the opportunity

for process improvement is infinite." Chrysler claims to have saved $400m by improving its supply-chain process.

2 It has a documented design, which is accessible to all. Electronic networks and the Internet are invaluable in disseminating process design around the organisation – so-called e-processing.

3 It is simple and flexible.

4 It compresses time. An insurance company, Aetna, for example, reduced the average time that it takes to handle a claim from 28 days to four hours.

5 It provides real-time feedback.

6 It has clear links with other processes.

7 It is customer-focused and user-friendly. Michael Hammer, whose writing is often vivid, wrote that: "A company that does not focus resolutely on its customers and the processes that produce value for its customers is not long for this world." Process improvements come from "walking in the customer's shoes", finding out what it is that customers really want, and then designing processes to meet that demand.

A brief history

The word process was traditionally associated with repetition, conjuring up images of desk-high binders detailing the minutiae of process flows. The goal of process design was to come up with the best possible process that could be repeated in exactly the same way every time.

Only in the 1990s did the idea escape from this straitjacket. Tom Davenport's 1992 book on the subject put information technology at the centre of process improvement. Only a challenge like process innovation, he went so far as to suggest, could give full scope to it's potential.

The concept of process excellence links two ideas that were current in the decade before Davenport's book. These were the idea of excellence (see page 89), propagated by Tom Peters and Robert Waterman in their best-selling book of 1982, and the ideas of Michael Porter about how firms gain competitive advantage (see page 35). Behind competitive advantage lay a fresh way of looking at a firm as a series of activities, linking together into what Porter called a value chain. Several writers went on from there to develop concepts based on the idea of a linked chain of activities (or processes).

Michael Porter himself has said that the ideas about processes sit comfortably with his own activity-based theories.

The literature on re-engineering employs the term processes.
Sometimes it is a synonym for activities. Sometimes it refers
to activities or sets of activities that cut across
organisational units. In any case, however, the essential
notion is the same – both strategic and operational issues
are best understood at the activity level.

By 1997 Hammer took the view that: "Processes are the key organisational theme for companies in the 21st century. Excellence in processes is what is going to distinguish successful organisations from the also-rans." He added, mindful of the main beneficiaries of most novel business ideas: "Capability at helping companies to achieve process excellence is what's going to distinguish leading consulting companies from those sweeping up after the elephants."

Recommended reading

Davenport, T., *Process Innovation, Re-engineering Work through Information Technology*, Harvard Business School Press, 1992
Hammer, M., "Re-engineering Work: Don't Automate, Obliterate", *Harvard Business Review*, July-August 1990
Building Process Excellence, Lessons from the Leaders, The Economist Intelligence Unit, 1996

Product life cycle

This is the idea that all products have a birth, life and death, and that they should be financed and marketed with this in mind. Even as a new product is being launched, its manufacturer should be preparing for the day when it has to be killed off. Its sales and profits start at a low level, rise (it is hoped) to a high level and then decline again to a low level. Sometimes this cycle is simply referred to in marketing circles as PLC.

Philip Kotler, one of the world's leading authorities on marketing, breaks the product life cycle into five distinct phases.

1 **Product development.** The phase when a company looks for a new product. New products do not have to be "out-of-the-blue" new (like the video-cassette recorder or the compact disc). They may be merely additions to existing product lines (the first cigarette with a filter tip, for instance) or improvements to existing products (a new whiter-than-white washing powder).
2 **Introduction.** The product's costs rise sharply as the heavy expense of advertising and marketing any new product begin to take their toll.
3 **Growth.** As the product begins to be accepted by the market, the company starts to recoup the costs of the first two phases.
4 **Maturity.** By now the product is widely accepted and growth slows down. Before long, however, a successful product in this phase will come under pressure from competition. The producer will have to start to spend again in order to defend the product's market position.
5 **Decline.** The company will no longer be able to fend off the competition, or some change in consumer tastes or lifestyle will render the product redundant. At this point the company has to decide how to bring the product's life to an end – what is the best end-game that it can play? (See also Game theory, page 100.)

Although managers know that a new product will follow this cycle, they are not sure when each phase will start and for how long each one will last. Although some products appear to have been around for ever (Kellogg's corn flakes, for example, or Kodak cameras) the products that bear these names today are entirely different from the ones that carried the same brand 50 years ago. The continuity of the brand name helps to disguise the fact that the product itself has been through several life cycles.

Products of fashion, by definition, have a shorter life cycle, and they thus have a much shorter time in which to reap their reward. A distinction is sometimes made between fashion items, such as clothing, and pure fads, such as pet rocks. It is not always immediately obvious into which of these two categories a product falls. When they were first introduced in the early 1980s, in-line skates seemed as if they might be a brief fad. But 20 years later they were still selling strongly, firmly set in the mature stage of their life cycle. They may not be destined for the life cycle of the corn flake, but they have already outlived many seemingly more permanent fashions.

Recommended reading

Kotler, P., *Marketing Management*, Prentice Hall (9th edition), 1997

Schewe, C.D. and Watson Hiam, A., *The Portable MBA in Marketing*, John Wiley (2nd edition), 1998

Treacy, M. and Wiersema, F., *The Discipline of Market Leaders*, Addison-Wesley, 1995

Quality circle

According to the *Quality Circles Handbook,*

> A quality circle is *a small group of between three and 12*
> *people who do the same or similar work, voluntarily*
> *meeting together regularly for about one hour per week in*
> *paid time, usually under the leadership of their own*
> *supervisor, and trained to identify, analyse and solve some*
> *of the problems in their work, presenting solutions to*
> *management and, where possible, implementing solutions*
> *themselves.*

It is a system, first introduced by a number of large Japanese firms, that aims to involve all the firm's employees, at every level, in an organisation's drive for quality.

There are two main parts to a quality circle's task: the identification of problems; and the suggestion of solutions. A secondary aim is to boost the morale of the group through attending the meetings and by being given a formal opportunity to discuss work-related issues.

Meetings are held in an organised way with a chairman being appointed on a rotating basis and an agenda prepared. Minutes are also taken. They serve as a useful means of following up proposals and the implementation of them.

The success of quality circles has been found to depend crucially on the amount of support that they get from the senior management of the firm, and on the amount of training that the participants are given in the ways and aims of the circles.

A brief history

Kaoru Ishikawa, a professor at Tokyo University who died in 1989, is attributed with much of the development of the idea of quality circles. They created great excitement in the West in the 1980s, at a time when every Japanese management technique was treated with great respect. Many firms in Europe and the United States set them up, including Westinghouse and Hewlett-Packard. It was claimed at one time in the 1980s that there were as many as 10m people participating in quality circles in Japanese industry alone.

However, the method also suffered a good deal of criticism. Even Joseph Juran, one of the two American post-war germinators of the quality ideal (the other was W. Edwards Deming), considered that quality circles were pretty useless if the company's management was not trained in the more general principles of total quality management (see page 225).

Others criticised the way in which the idea was transferred from one culture to another without any attempt to tailor it to suit local traditions. It may, they suggested, be well suited to Japan's participative workforce, but in more individualistic western societies it frequently became a formalised hunt for someone to blame for the problems that it identified. The original intention was that it should be a collective search for a solution to those problems.

The idea of quality circles fell from grace as they were seen to be failing to live up to their promise. A study made in 1988 found that 80% of a sample of large companies in the West that had introduced quality circles in the early 1980s had abandoned them before the end of the decade.

In his book *Quality, a Critical Introduction*, John Beckford quotes the example of a western retailer that took almost every wrong step in the book. These included:

- training only managers to run quality circles, and not the staff in the retail outlets who were expected to participate in them;
- setting up circles where managers appointed themselves as leaders and made their secretaries keep the minutes. This maintained the existing hierarchy which quality circles are supposed to break out of;
- expecting staff to attend meetings outside working hours and without pay;
- ignoring real problems raised by the staff (about, for example, the outlets' opening hours) and focusing on trivia (were there enough ashtrays in the customer reception area).

Recommended reading

Beckford, J., *Quality, a Critical Introduction*, Routledge, 1998
Crosby, P., *Quality is Free*, Mentor, 1979
Hutchins, D., *Quality Circles Handbook*, Pitman, 1985
Ishikawa, K., *What is Total Quality Control?*, Prentice Hall, 1985
Juran, J., *Juran on Planning for Quality*, Free Press, 1988

Re-engineering

The idea of re-engineering was first propounded in an article in the *Harvard Business Review* of July-August 1990 by Michael Hammer, a professor of computer science at MIT. It promised a novel approach to corporate change, and was described by its inventors as a "fundamental rethinking and radical redesign of business processes to achieve dramatic improvements in critical measures of performance such as cost, quality, service and speed".

The technique involved analysing a company's central processes and reassembling them in a more efficient fashion and in a way that rode roughshod over long-established (but frequently irrelevant) functional distinctions. Functional silos were often protective of information, for instance, and of their own position in the scheme of things. At best, this was inefficient. Slicing the silos into their different processes and reassembling them in a less vertical fashion exposed excess fat and forced corporations to look at new ways to streamline themselves.

The method was frequently referred to as business process re-engineering (popularly known as BPR). But its creators, Michael Hammer and James Champy, aspired for greater things. They maintained that re-engineering had a wider significance than mere processes. It applied to all parts of an organisation, and it had a lofty purpose. "I think that this is the work of angels," said Hammer in one of his more fanciful moments. "In a world where so many people are so deprived, it's a sin to be so inefficient."

Many commentators, however, saw re-engineering as a return to the mechanistic ideas of Frederick Taylor (see Scientific management, page 193). Others saw it as a shallow intellectual justification for downsizing (see page 71), a process of slimming down that was being forced on many corporations by developments in information technology.

One of the faults of the idea, which the creators themselves acknowledged, was that re-engineering became something that managers were only too happy to impose on others but not on themselves. Champy's follow-up book was pointedly called *Re-engineering Management*. "If their jobs and styles are left largely intact, managers will eventually undermine the very structure of their rebuilt enterprises," he wrote with considerable foresight in 1994.

A brief history

The idea of re-engineering was developed in the early 1990s by Michael Hammer and James Champy, head of the CSC management consultancy. It followed a classic route for popular management ideas: from a university academic's research, via a management consultancy's marketing and a best-selling book, into (briefly) a perceived panacea for all companies' ills. This is something, of course, that neither it nor any other management fad has ever actually been. It was helped by the fact that the book's authors (Hammer in particular) were eminently quotable.

It was implemented with considerable success by a number of high-profile organisations. The Hallmark card company, for instance, completely re-engineered its new-product process; and Kodak's re-engineering of its black-and-white film manufacturing process cut the firm's response time to new orders in half.

By the mid-1990s, however, the phrase BPR had come to be closely associated with the redundancies that seemed to be its inevitable accompaniment. Because of this, CSC subtly changed the name of the service that it offered to BPI (business process improvement). In BPI, processes could be improved without necessarily involving lay-offs.

The idea of re-engineering processes was given a boost by the development of ERP (see Enterprise resource planning, page 82). ERP systems enabled a firm's different operations to talk to each other electronically. At last the left hand of the organisation knew what the right hand was up to, and processes which sliced horizontally across the organisation's different operations could be redesigned from scratch.

Recommended reading

Champy, J. and Hammer, M., *Re-engineering the Corporation*, HarperBusiness, 1993

Champy, J., *Re-engineering Management: the Mandate for New Leadership*, Harper Business, 1995

Hammer, M., "Re-engineering Work: Don't Automate, Obliterate", *Harvard Business Review*, July-August 1990

Hammer, M. and Stanton, S., *The Re-engineering Revolution*, HarperCollins, 1995

Satisficing

This is the idea that individuals do not (as classic economic theory would have it) seek to maximise their benefit from a particular course of action, but rather that they seek something that is good enough; that is, satisfactory. This process, described as satisficing, has great relevance for consumers when faced with shop-shelf decisions. Do they hunt around assiduously until they find the best deal? Or do they settle for more or less the first thing that seems adequate?

The idea is based on a view of the limitations of the human mind and was developed by Herbert Simon, an American professor of computer science and psychology, in the 1960s. He maintained that individuals cannot possibly consider all the alternatives available to them. Not only can they not get access to all the information required, but even if they could, their minds would be unable to process it properly. Hence the human mind restricts itself. It is, as Simon put it, bounded by "cognitive limits". This presents a problem for classical economists for whom consumers are always in search of the best.

Simon suggested that humans, when in buying mode, have an aspiration level, which they consider acceptable although not necessarily optimal. They then search through a limited number of options in sequence. When they come across one that meets their aspiration level they go for it. "Whereas economic man maximises, selects the best alternative from among all those available to him; his cousin, administrative man, satisfices, looks for a course of action that is satisfactory or 'good enough'," he wrote. Examples of satisficing in everyday business life are things like an adequate profit and a fair price.

Simon went on to say:

> Because he satisfices rather than maximises, administrative
> man can make his choices without first examining all
> possible behaviour alternatives, and without ascertaining
> that these are in fact all the alternatives. Second, because he
> treats the world as rather empty and ignores the
> interrelatedness of all things (so stupefying to thought and
> action), administrative man can make decisions with
> relatively simple rules of thumb that do not make
> impossible demands upon his capacity for thought.

Hence big businesses can be run by small minds, but big economies (maybe) cannot.

One of the most powerful supporters of the idea of satisficing is common sense. It "fits pretty well our introspective knowledge of our own judgmental processes as well as the more formal descriptions of those processes made by the psychologists who have studied them", argued Simon.

A brief history

The idea of satisficing has been applied in many different contexts. In particular, it has been shown to influence the way in which people answer survey questionnaires. Respondents often choose satisfactory answers rather than searching for an optimum answer. Satisficing of this kind can dramatically distort the traditional statistical analysis of market research.

The idea has also been applied to managers when solving problems. All the options presented by any particular situation cannot be known to them, so they limit themselves to a small number that are. They then choose one that seems to them satisfactory (although it is inevitably less than perfect). Likewise, a company's strategy may be determined in the same way.

Take this a step further, and it suggests that every firm's competitors are merely satisficing, that is, putting in a level of performance that is satisfactory but far from optimal. Thus industry benchmarks (see page 8) may not show anything like best practice, but merely acceptable practice.

Recommended reading

March, J.G. and Simon, H.A., *Organisations*, John Wiley, 1958
Simon, H.A., *Administrative Behaviour*, The Free Press (3rd edition), 1976

Scenario planning

Scenario planning is a fun way for organisations to think about the future. A group of executives sets out to draw a small number of scenarios, stories about how the future may unfold and how this might affect an issue that confronts them. The issue could be a narrow one: whether to make a particular investment, for example. Should a supermarket chain put millions into more out-of-town megastores and their attendant car parks, or should it invest in secure websites and a chain of vans to make door-to-door deliveries? Or it could be much wider: a US education authority, for instance, contemplating the impact of demographic change on the need for new schools. Will the ageing of the population be counterbalanced by the rising level of immigration?

In Peter Schwartz's book *The Art of the Long View*, scenarios are described as:

> *Stories that can help us recognise and adapt to changing aspects of our present environment. They form a method for articulating the different pathways that might exist for you tomorrow, and finding your appropriate movements down each of those possible paths. Scenario planning is about making choices today with an understanding of how they might turn out.*

The process of scenario planning is a structured one. It usually begins with a long discussion about how the executives think that big shifts in society, economics, politics and technology might affect the issue under discussion. From this the group aims to draw up a list of priorities, including things that will have the most impact on the issue under discussion and those whose outcome is the most uncertain. These priorities then form the basis for sketching out rough pictures of the future.

At further meetings, preferably after they have had a night to sleep on it, the executives flesh out the scenarios. At the same time, they attempt to identify some early warning signals – things that, should they happen, would be strong indicators that one particular scenario was beginning to unfold (in the real world) rather than any other. For instance, if Levi's experiment with computer-designed tailored jeans were a huge success it might suggest that consumers were moving away from price-driven mass markets to a world of more personalised, less price-sensitive products.

The executives undertaking the exercise are encouraged to fantasise and stretch their imaginations. This involves persuading them to ask outrageous "What if?" questions. In the 1980s, for example, scenario planning compelled the Pentagon to think about the consequences of the end of the cold war long before anybody imagined that it would actually end in their lifetime. When the oil price was at rock bottom in the early 1970s, scenario planners at Royal Dutch Shell forced its board to think of the consequences of an overnight quadrupling of the oil price well before OPEC actually made that happen. The company's forethought is credited with helping Shell to emerge from the oil-market turmoil of the 1970s in better shape than its rivals.

Scenario planning draws on a wide range of disciplines and interests, including economics, psychology, politics and demographics. The recommended reading list of Global Business Network, a leading adviser on scenario planning, includes Alexis de Tocqueville's *Democracy in America* as well as Peter Senge's *The Fifth Discipline* and *The Leopard*, Giuseppe Tomasi's sweeping tale of Sicilian family life.

A brief history

Scenario planning grew out of the thinking of a number of leading companies in the early 1970s (particularly Royal Dutch Shell) about the corporate planning function. They were driven by a combination of two things.

- Widespread dissatisfaction with existing ways of planning for the future. Many organisations had come to realise how misleading were the predictions based on straight-line extrapolations from the past. The oil price hikes of 1973 and 1978 dramatically and painfully brought home how vulnerable businesses were to sudden discontinuities in their markets. The unusually smooth path of economic progress since the second world war had lulled them into a false sense of continuity.
- Growing attachment to the idea that business can make better use of the non-rational side of human nature. At the head of Shell's planning department at the time was Pierre Wack, a Belgian who had been persuaded to give up the editorship of a Franco-German philosophy magazine in order to join the company.

In an article in the *Harvard Business Review* in 1985 Wack wrote:

> *Scenarios deal with two worlds; the world of facts and the world of perceptions. They explore for facts but they aim at perceptions inside the heads of decision-makers. Their purpose is to gather and transform information of strategic significance into fresh perceptions. This transformation process is not trivial – more often than not it does not happen. When it works, it is a creative experience that generates a heartfelt "Aha" ... and leads to strategic insights beyond the mind's reach.*

Scenario planning is a way of injecting the "Aha" factor into business planning. It has been (and continues to be) used by some of the world's largest corporations, including Royal Dutch Shell, Motorola, IBM, AT&T, Disney and Andersen Consulting.

Recommended reading

Schwartz, P., *The Art of the Long View*, John Wiley, 1996
Wack, P., "The Gentle Art of Re-perceiving", *Harvard Business Review*, September-October, 1985

Scientific management

Scientific management was the first big management idea to reach a mass audience. It swept through corporate America in the early years of the 20th century. Much management thinking since has been either a reaction to the idea of scientific management, or a development of it.

The idea was first propounded by Frederick Winslow Taylor, an American Quaker whose tombstone in Pennsylvania bears the inscription "The Father of Scientific Management". Like many management theorists after him, Taylor first trained as an engineer.

Scientific management was developed in response to a motivational problem, which at the time was called "soldiering" – the attempt among workers to do the least amount of work in the longest amount of time. To counter this, Taylor proposed that managers should scientifically measure productivity and set high targets for workers to achieve. This was in contrast to the alternative method, known as initiative and incentive, in which workers were rewarded with higher wages or promotion. Taylor described this method as "poisonous".

Scientific management required managers to walk around with stop watches and note pads carrying out time-and-motion studies on workers in different departments. It led to the piece-rate system in which workers were paid for their output, not for their time.

Taylor believed that "the principal object of management should be to secure the maximum prosperity for the employer, coupled with the maximum prosperity of each employee". The interests of management, workers and owners were thus intertwined. He wanted to remove "all possible brain work" from the shop floor, handing all action, as far as possible, over to machines. "In the past, the man has been first; in the future the machine must be first," he was fond of saying. He ignited a debate about man versus machine that continued far into the 20th century.

A brief history

Taylor started his career at the Midvale Steel Works where he became chief engineer before moving to the Bethlehem Steel Company. There he first carried out experiments to prove the validity of scientific management. He broke down manual tasks into a series of components that could be measured, and he subsequently showed them to have improved and resulted in greater productivity at the plant.

The famous book in which he enunciated his theories, *The Principles of Scientific Management*, had a strong impact on subsequent management thinking. It influenced, for instance, people like Frank and Lillian Gilbreth, American time-and-motion experts; industrial psychologists, many of whom saw it as an insult to the human spirit and set out to show that allowing free rein to human initiative produced far superior results; and industrialists like the Michelin brothers (of tyre fame). Even Lenin at one time exhorted Marxist workers to "try out every scientific and progressive suggestion of the Taylor system".

The trade union movement, however, always hated it. One union officer said: "No tyrant or slave driver in the ecstasy of his most delirious dream ever sought to place upon abject slaves a condition more repugnant". Peter Drucker once wrote that Taylor was "the first man in history who did not take work for granted, but looked at it and studied it. His approach to work is still the basic foundation".

There is little space for Taylor's ideas in today's world of freewheeling teamwork. But some consider the writings of people like Michael Porter and Michael Hammer, with their focus on breaking businesses down into measurable (and controllable) activities, to have more than a faint echo of Taylor's mechanistic theories.

Recommended reading

Gilbreth, F.B., *Primer of Scientific Management*, D. Van Nostrand, 1912

Taylor, F.W., *A Piece-Rate System*, 1895

Taylor, F.W., *The Principles of Scientific Management*, Harper and Brothers, 1911

Urwick, L. and Brech, E.F.L., *The Making of Scientific Management*, Management Publications Trust, 1946

Worthy, J., *Big Business and Free Men*, Harper & Row, 1959

Segmentation

Segmentation is the process of slicing the market for a particular product or service into a number of different segments. One segment of the market for video cameras, for example, is the group of people with new-born babies. Another is the group of people visiting relatives who live abroad.

Once they have identified different segments of their market in this way, manufacturers can then target their marketing and advertising efforts more accurately and more profitably. Different segments can be reached through the most appropriate channel: parents of new-borns through magazines designed for them or through ante-natal clinics, for instance. Broadcasting the claims of a brand or product to an undifferentiated public is not always very effective.

Each market segment represents a bunch of potential customers with common characteristics. In consumer markets, segmentation is usually based on the following.

- **Demographic factors.** Gender, age, family size, and so on.
- **Geography.** In most countries there are marked differences in the consumer preferences of different regions. The consumption of wine in the north of England, for example, is very different from that in the south.
- **Social factors.** The classic segmentation is by income and occupation, but this is proving to be less and less useful. There are a lot of extremely wealthy people who do not spend much, and vice versa. So the focus is shifting to lifestyle. At the end of the 20th century, marketers became more interested in categorising consumers as "generation xers" or "third agers" than by the size of their bank accounts.

Industrial markets have been notoriously more difficult to segment than consumer markets. Firms find it hard to decide which factors are useful for categorising their corporate clients. Should it be size, industry sector, or geography? Computer maker Hewlett-Packard has segmented its big industrial customers into five different categories based on the value of the companies' purchases and on the complexity of their systems. The categories are as follows.

- Big spenders with complex systems.
- Small spenders with complex systems that might be moved into the first category.
- Big spenders with simple systems.
- Small spenders with complex systems that cannot be moved into the first category, such as small, high-tech businesses.
- Small spenders with simple systems.

A brief history

The idea of segmentation had its heyday in the 1960s and 1970s. It was a reaction against the mass-marketing tactics sparked off by Henry Ford when he said that customers could buy his Model T car "in any colour as long as it's black".

Many of its classifications, however, have proved to be less and less useful. Baby boomers have been found to have little in common other than their defining characteristic: a birthdate in the years immediately after the second world war. As John Forsyth, a consultant, wrote in the *McKinsey Quarterly* in 1999: "Unfortunately, easy cases permitting marketers to establish meaningful differences among groups of customers and then to identify them – a phenomenon we call 'actionable segmentation' – are rare."

In the 1990s there was a reversal of the tendency to be more and more precise about identifying particular segments. Mobil, an oil company, for example, found that only 20% of the customers for its petrol were price sensitive. But instead of trying to identify them and give them special offers, it went for the 80% who were not price sensitive and shifted its marketing focus away from providing the lowest price at the pumps. The company says it earned an extra $118m in a year as a result.

The increasing use of the Internet has provided new opportunities for segmentation. It offers continuous opportunities to capture information about customer behaviour. Consumers identify themselves and their characteristics by their electronic participation in particular interest groups, and by their general online behaviour. For many marketers, this has presented the prospect of what has become known as the market of one, a separate market for each individual consumer. The market of one, of course, is also the segment of one.

The ultimate step in segmentation will not just be a focus on individual customers themselves, however, but on individual customers at specific moments in time. People who eat "Bisko" cereals at the rate of a packet every 22–23 days will then be approached to buy another packet after their breakfast on the 20th day; not before and not after.

Recommended reading

Forsyth, J. et al, "A Segmentation You Can Act On", *McKinsey Quarterly*, No. 3, 1999

Shapiro, P.B. and Bonoma, T.V., "How to Segment Industrial Markets", *Harvard Business Review*, January-February 1984

The Seven Ss

The Seven Ss is the name of a framework developed in the late 1970s and early 1980s for analysing organisations and looking at the various elements that make them successful (or not). The framework has seven aspects, each of them beginning with the letter S, hence the mnemonic.

1 Strategy: the route that the organisation has chosen for its future growth.
2 Structure: the way in which the organisation is put together; how its different bits relate to each other.
3 Systems: the formal and informal procedures that govern everyday activity; today this increasingly involves the implementation of information technology.
4 Skills: the distinctive capabilities of the people who work for the organisation.
5 Shared values: originally called superordinate goals, the things that influence a group to work together for a common aim.
6 Staff: the organisation's human resources.
7 Style: the way in which the organisation's employees present themselves to the outside world, to suppliers and customers.

The Seven Ss helped to change managers' thinking about how companies could be improved. The theory told them that it was not just a matter of devising a new strategy and following it through (as they might have thought before). Nor was it a matter of setting up new systems and letting them generate improvements. To improve, companies had to pay attention to all seven of the Ss at the same time.

The seven were often subdivided into the first three (strategy, structure and systems), referred to as the hard Ss, and the last four, which were called the soft Ss. The theory was developed in the context of the astoundingly rapid progress of Japanese manufacturing companies in the 1960s and 1970s. Western companies, it was said, were better at the hard Ss. But it was because the Japanese combined both hard and soft that they were so much more successful.

All seven are interrelated, so a change in one has a ripple effect on all the others. Hence it is impossible to make progress on one without making progress on all. For western firms, where the hard Ss receive the bulk of management's attention, this is a root cause of their under-performance.

Diagrammatically, the seven are represented in a circle to convey the idea that they are all of equal significance. No one of them is more important than any other, although the theory's champion, Richard Pascale, subsequently gave a special status to superordinate goals. These, he said, "provide the glue that holds the other six together". This positioning of superordinate goals at the centre of the circle stimulated some of the subsequent work on corporate culture (see page 51), since culture is in some sense a combination of an organisation's superordinate goals and its style.

A brief history

Just as the growth share matrix (see page 109) is powerfully associated with one of the two leading strategic consultancies (the Boston Consulting Group), so the Seven Ss is linked with the other (McKinsey & Co). It was the seedcorn from which grew the idea of excellence (see page 89) and the most popular business book ever written (*In Search of Excellence*). Excellent companies were those that excelled at all of the Seven Ss.

The authors of the book, Tom Peters and Robert Waterman, had worked with Richard Pascale in the late 1970s and early 1980s to develop the idea of the Seven Ss. Pascale subsequently expounded the idea in his book *The Art of Japanese Management*, in which he compared the Japanese company Matsushita with the American company ITT, greatly to the credit of the former.

Recommended reading

Pascale, R. and Athos, A., *The Art of Japanese Management*, Simon & Schuster, 1981

Small is beautiful

Small is Beautiful is perhaps the most famous title of any business book ever written. But it was not the title that was originally conceived by its author, E.F. Schumacher. It was added as a last-minute afterthought by his publisher. The book's subtitle is the less engaging A *Study of Economics as if People Mattered*. In many ways the main title is misleading, for the book is not a paean in praise of smallness. It is more a polemic against industry's crude brutality and (among other things) its despoiling of the environment and of the human spirit. Its frontispiece quotes a historian, R.H. Tawney:

> *Since even quite common men have souls, no increase in material wealth will compensate them for arrangements which insult their self-respect and impair their freedom. A reasonable estimate of economic organisation must allow for the fact that, unless industry is to be paralysed by recurrent revolts on the part of outraged human nature, it must satisfy criteria which are not purely economic.*

If a more caring industry and "the humanisation of work" could be achieved only by breaking big firms up into a number of small firms, then (in Schumacher's schema) small would, indeed, be beautiful. But Schumacher never attempted to show that meanness of spirit bears any relationship to the size of the organisation in which it is being exercised.

A brief history

The catchphrase "small is beautiful" became popular after industrial gigantism had been the dominant trend for much of the 20th century, fuelled partly by the need for industry to satisfy the thirst of two world wars. With the wars well ended, it was time for a swing of the pendulum.

After the book was written, a number of countries set up government bodies to look at ways in which the disadvantages that small firms faced, particularly in financial markets, might be removed. As a result, a number of schemes, such as low-interest loans and subsidised office accommodation, were established for small firms.

Schumacher himself was a German economist who spent much of his working life in a large organisation, the UK's National Coal Board. His experience there led him to believe that large corporations were successful only when they tried to behave like a number of small ones. He wrote:

> *Organisations should imitate nature, which doesn't allow a single cell to become too large ... The fundamental task is to achieve smallness within large organisations ... The great achievement of Mr Sloan of General Motors was to structure this gigantic firm in such a manner that it became in fact a federation of fairly reasonably sized firms.*

He also used the National Coal Board as an example of a big organisation that had set up a number of "quasi-firms" within it. These quasi-firms, he said, had to have a large amount of freedom "to give the greatest possible chance to creativity and entrepreneurship".

By the end of the 20th century it was large corporations that seemed in need of a Schumacher-style champion. By then many of the predominant economic forces had moved in favour of small companies. In 1999 businesses with fewer than 100 employees accounted for roughly two-thirds of all the jobs in the United States and one-third of its GNP. In some industries small firms were dominant: in the travel industry, for example, where half of all turnover in the industry in the United States was accounted for by firms with fewer than 100 employees.

At the same time, talented graduates increasingly preferred to work for small companies where they could have greater responsibility at a younger age and a piece of the action (in the shape of equity in their employer). Small companies were more flexible and more fun.

Put on the defensive, big companies began to look for new ways to compete with these upstarts. One way they found was to tap into the small companies' pool of talent by setting up joint ventures with them. This became a popular way, for instance, for large pharmaceuticals firms to gain access to the richest pools of postgraduate talent, talent which no longer automatically drifted their way.

Recommended reading

Davis, R. and Austerberry, T., "Think Small; Win Big", *McKinsey Quarterly*, No. 1, 1999
Schumacher, E.F., *Small is Beautiful*, Blond & Briggs, 1973

Span of control

The span of control is the number of people that can be effectively managed by any one manager. At one time it was thought that there was a single ideal span of control based on some fundamental human capacity. Zealous hunters after this number were spurred on by the thought that once unearthed it would be the key to the perfect corporation. Organisation charts could then be structured in a rigid and perfect manner for all time. Over the years, however, there have been so many differing views about the optimum size of the span of control that the unavoidable conclusion is that it is a question of horses for courses.

The ideal span is determined partly by the nature of the work involved. With craftsmen the number can be quite small because the level of supervision required is high. In mass production, however, the span of control can be ten times higher because each worker has a clearly defined task to perform, requiring little regular oversight.

The span of control can be deliberately enlarged by making workers more autonomous and more capable of managing themselves. It can also be enlarged by increasing the number of rules and further constraining the freedom of junior employees to make mistakes. As the span of control gets larger, it exponentially (and quite dramatically) increases the number of relationships between individuals within that management cell. One manager and six subordinates, for instance, creates 222 relationships among the seven of them; one manager and 16 subordinates creates over 500,000 relationships. This takes some managing.

In general, the smaller the span of control, the higher is the level of the organisation. This is because those at the top are not only responsible directly for the employees who report to them, but also (indirectly) for the lower-level employees who report to their underlings.

Managers were traditionally compensated according to the number of employees under their span of control. Their route to higher rewards was to move up the pyramid by climbing the corporate ladder. In the delayered organisations of the late 20th century this reward structure needed to be rethought.

A brief history

As long ago as the early 19th century, Eli Whitney was experimenting by giving managers different spans of control at his gun factory in the

United States. Almost 200 hundred years later the experiments are still continuing.

Views on the ideal span of control have been changing over time as the thinking about corporate structure itself has changed. For the first 60 years of the 20th century, managers favoured the command-and-control structure based largely on military models. Bosses needed to keep a tight watch on their underlings, so the ideal span could never be large. A consensus formed around the number six. This involved the construction of a steep pyramid with many layers of managers, each with six employees directly beneath them. Since the span of control and the number of layers within an organisation are interrelated, a low span of control creates a tall organisation (one with many layers) whereas a high span of control creates a flatter structure.

After 1960, however, management styles began to change, and command-and-control methods were increasingly deemed to be inefficient. Flatter, less hierarchical and more loosely structured organisations implied larger spans of control (see also Delayering, page 62). This time the consensus on the size of the ideal span fell somewhere between 15 and 25. There was also a widespread feeling that five layers was the maximum with which any large organisation could function effectively.

The coming of the virtual organisation (see page 235) made managers take a new look at the concept. In a virtual organisation there is little direct control. People work increasingly as independent self-contained units, either individually or as small teams. They have access to (electronic) information that lays down the boundaries within which they can be autonomous, but which at the same time allows them to be completely free within those boundaries. In such an environment, the ideal span of control can be very large. Indeed, it can scarcely be called a span of control any more; it is more a span of loose links and alliances.

Strategic alliance

A strategic alliance is a relationship between two or more organisations that falls somewhere between the extremes of an arm's-length sourcing arrangement and a full-blown acquisition. It embraces franchising, licensing and joint ventures.

Booz Allen & Hamilton, a firm of management consultants that is an acknowledged leader in the field, defines a strategic alliance as:

> A co-operative arrangement between two or more companies in which:
> - a common strategy is developed in unison and a win-win attitude is adopted by all parties;
> - the relationship is reciprocal, with each partner prepared to share specific strengths with the other, thus lending power to the enterprise;
> - a pooling of resources, investment and risks occurs for mutual gain.

In general, there are two types of strategic alliance: a bilateral alliance (between two organisations); and a network alliance (between several organisations). The alliance between Bank of Scotland and Tesco whereby the British supermarket chain provided the Scottish bank's services throughout its stores was an example of the former; the Airbus consortium and the Visa card network are examples of the latter.

Strategic alliances have many advantages: they involve little immediate financial commitment; they allow companies to put their toes into new markets before they get soaked; and they offer a quiet retreat should a venture not work out as the partners had hoped. But going into something knowing that it is (literally) not a big deal, and that there is a face-saving exit route built in, may not be the best way to make the people charged with running it hungry for success.

The most popular use for alliances is as a means to put a toe into a foreign market. Not surprisingly, therefore, there are more alliances in Europe and Asia (where there are more foreign markets) than in the United States. In some cases, alliances have been used by companies because other means of entering a market are closed to them. Hence there have been many in the airline industry where governments are sensitive about their domestic carriers falling into foreign hands; for example, the oneworld alliance which brings together Aer Lingus, AA, BA, Canadian Airlines, Cathay Pacific, Finnair, Iberia and Qantas and the Star Alliance linking Lufthansa with Air Canada, Air New Zealand, All Nippon Airways, Ansett Australia, SAS, Thai Airways, United and Varig.

One thing considered to be crucial to a successful alliance is a certain degree of cultural compatibility. For example, companies are advised to pick on someone their own size. Alliances between the very big and the very small are hard to operate because of the different significance that the alliance assumes in each organisation's scale of things.

Alliances are often said to be much like marriages. The partners have to understand each other's expectations, be sensitive to each other's changes of mood and not be too surprised if their partnership ends in divorce. Indeed, many companies build into their alliances a sort of pre-nuptial contract, an agreement as to what is to happen to their joint property in the event of a subsequent divorce.

A brief history

Strategic alliances grew at a phenomenal rate in the 1990s. Some companies, such as General Electric and AT&T, set up several hundred. On one estimate, IBM cemented almost 1,000 strategic alliances during the decade. Booz Allen & Hamilton reckons that more than 20,000 were formed worldwide in the period 1996-98. Andersen Consulting says that Fortune 500 companies have an average of 50–70 alliances each.

Alliances were once confined to small non-central parts of an organisation's business. But not any more. In 1998 BT and AT&T agreed to bundle their international assets into a single joint venture that started off with an annual revenue of $11 billion, an annual operating profit of $1 billion and some 5,000 employees. AT&T has an alliance with Microsoft that is designed to deliver broadband services via cable TV networks, not a business that either partner envisages as being on the margin.

By the end of the 20th century strategic alliances were seen by many companies as their main engine for growth. The other two ways for a company to grow, organically or through mergers and acquisitions, had run out of steam in many markets. In this environment, the management of its network of alliances becomes a key skill for the corporation.

Recommended reading

Harrigan, K., Strategies for Declining Businesses, Lexington Books, 1980

Strategic planning

In ancient Greek, the word στρατηγια meant the art of generalship, of devising and carrying out a military campaign. The English word derived from it, strategy, was transferred from its military origins to the business world in the years before the ubiquitous MBA, at a time when a military career was considered to be the ideal qualification for a manager. As with the military, strategy was seen by business as a high-level function fit only for the mind of the supreme leader and a small cohort of the brightest and best. The planning of corporate strategy was usually a secretive operation that took place at irregular intervals.

Although the problems of strategic planning attracted some of the best minds, in both business and academia, these minds could not agree on a best practice that would work in all circumstances. Most people could agree with the general guidelines laid down by Alfred Chandler, namely, that strategic planning involves the articulation of some long-term goals and the allocation of the necessary resources to achieve these goals. But beyond that there were few common themes.

Igor Ansoff pointed out a crucial distinction between strategic planning and what he called strategic management. Strategic management has three parts:

- strategic planning;
- the skill of a firm in converting its plans into reality; and
- the skill of a firm in managing its own internal resistance to change.

Ansoff's analysis was based on his observation that "as firms became increasingly skilful strategy formulators, the translation of strategy into results in the market place lagged behind. This created paralysis by analysis in strategic planning", and in many firms it led to the suppression of strategic planning.

Henry Mintzberg identified ten different schools of thought about strategic planning, and then ducked out of choosing between them by saying that the term was a misnomer because it simply formalised strategies that already existed. Strategies, he maintained, were visions not plans.

A brief history

In the 1960s the popularity of strategic planning gave a big boost to the fledgling management consulting business. As *Business Week* wrote, it "spawned a mini-industry of brainy consulting boutiques ... you could plot a strategy that would safely steer your company to uninterrupted triumph if only you thought hard enough". New firms such as the Boston Consulting Group grew rapidly as a result of success with strategic ideas such as the growth share matrix (see page 109) and the experience curve (see page 92). Older firms such as McKinsey also grew rapidly as a result of their skill at strategic planning.

By the 1980s, however, strategic planning had gone out of fashion. As companies drew in their belts (first because of global competition, particularly from the Japanese, and then because of recession) they found that their strategic planning departments (which inevitably employed high-powered and expensive people) could be axed quite painlessly. Future growth (and the planning of that growth) was not on the agenda. Corporations focused more narrowly on improving the returns on the assets that they already held. This inevitably involved the introduction of information technology, and IT required a more technical type of consultant than the polished presenters from BCG and McKinsey.

General Electric led the way when it axed its respected planning department in 1983. GE's chief executive at the time, Jack Welch, felt that the department's 200 or more senior executives were too involved with financial minutiae and not enough with new businesses and visionary markets. GE's strategic planning was passed on to the bosses of its 12 main business units, and thereafter they met every summer for full-day sessions on strategy. They looked at both the short-term horizon and four years ahead.

It was not until the mid-1990s that strategic planning began to stage a revival. *Business Week* put the event on its cover in August 1996. "After a decade of gritty downsizing," it wrote, "Big Thinkers are back in corporate vogue." There were two fundamental reasons for this.

- Corporations, especially American ones, were beginning to think about growth again.
- The arrival of the Internet and the possibilities of e-commerce (see page 74) were compelling companies to think carefully about where they wanted to go in the new electronic business world. Companies such as Disney, for instance, appointed senior executives specifically in charge of strategic planning for their online businesses.

On its reappearance, however, strategic planning took a different form. It was a continuous process, not (as it had been) a discrete half-yearly or annual coven attended by a select few. Nokia, a mobile phone company, says it is aiming to make strategy "a daily part of a manager's activity". It also began to involve many more people, both inside and outside the organisation. Hewlett-Packard, for example, brought both customers and suppliers together with general managers in its strategic planning sessions. EDS involved over 2,000 of its employees in a late 1990s strategic planning process. But Gary Hamel, one of the new-age strategy gurus, still found it "amazing that young people who live closest to the future are the most disenfranchised in strategy-creating exercises".

Recommended reading

Ansoff, I., *Corporate Strategy*, McGraw-Hill, 1965

Chandler, A., *Strategy and Structure*, MIT Press, 1962

Hamel, G., "Strategy as Revolution", *Harvard Business Review*, July-August 1996

Mintzberg, H., "Crafting Strategy", *Harvard Business Review* July-August 1987

Porter, M., "What is Strategy?", *Harvard Business Review*, November-December 1996

Structure

The classification of corporate structures, and the search for the optimum structure for organisations, has fascinated business academics over the years. A German social scientist, Max Weber, took the subject away from a dry examination of formal lines of authority and made it into a study of how people actually behave within organisations. His classic work, *The Theory of Social and Economic Organisation*, describes three phases of structure. First there is the charismatic stage, the time when the organisation relies on a single leader's vision and example. Then comes the traditional organisation, where rules are established and precedents set. Lastly, there is the bureaucratic stage, where everything is run with machine-like efficiency. The military is an example of an organisation in this third stage.

A Canadian professor, Henry Mintzberg, devised another influential classification. He identified five basic structures.

1 **The simple structure.** This is the young company before its entrepreneurial founder has had to let go of some of the strings. It is often autocratic and, as Mintzberg points out, vulnerable to a single heart attack. Before the industrial revolution it was the only structure around.

2 **The machine bureaucracy.** This is the company with many layers of management and a mass of formal procedures. It is slow to react to change and seems ill-equipped for the 21st century.

3 **The professional bureaucracy.** This is the organisation that is cemented together by some sort of professional expertise, such as a hospital or a consultancy. It is usually the most democratic, partly because it is often set up as a partnership. The decisions, like the profits, are shared.

4 **The divisionalised form.** This is the machine bureaucracy that has shed much of its bureaucracy. It is a structure where there is little central authority, but whatever there is is clearly defined.

5 **The adhocracy.** This is the type of organisation frequently found in the computer world, full of flexible teams working on specific projects. It is also the structure found in Hollywood and, says Mintzberg, it is the structure of the future.

Mintzberg's classification embraces a fundamental distinction between organisations that are vertical (types 1, 2 and 4) and those that are horizontal (types 3 and 5).

In his book, *The Horizontal Organisation*, Frank Ostroff defines the vertical structure as one:

> ... *with multiple reporting levels and a decision-making apparatus that concentrates authority near the top. "Thinking" is delegated to management; "doing" is accomplished in a collection of functionally distinct departments populated by individuals who are focused on specialised and generally fragmented tasks.*

Historically, most organisations have been organised vertically. This structure was well suited to the Industrial Revolution and the needs of mass production. But the Information Age is believed to require something different. The modern organisation needs a workforce with a much higher degree of average skills. It also needs to be much more focused on the customer (on titillating demand rather than on optimising supply). These requirements, it is argued, are best met by a horizontal structure.

Horizontal organisations have a number of defining features.

- They make teams, not individuals, the central unit of organisational design.
- They are built around cross-functional core processes, not around tasks or functions.
- They are much closer to their customers and their suppliers.
- They create a corporate culture of openness and co-operation.

A brief history

The idea that an organisation's structure is not something that can be designed and considered in the abstract was stimulated by Alfred Chandler's 1962 business classic, *Strategy and Structure*. He argued that all successful companies must have a structure that matches their strategy. An economic historian, Chandler based his theory on studies of large American corporations between the years 1850 and 1920, when companies were developing from single-unit, centrally managed operations into umbrella-type structures where a number of comparatively autonomous units shared certain overheads, in particular the strategic planning function. He found the origins of modern management hierarchies in the rapid growth of the American railroads. Local decision-making was required on and near the track, but at the same time there was a need for a headquarters to co-ordinate all the local operations. The structure was forced on to the organisations by outside events.

In recent years, outside events (in particular globalisation and the growing importance of information technology) have again forced many businesses to rethink their structure. Companies as different as General Electric, Ford, Motorola, Xerox and Barclays have adopted horizontal structures to varying degrees.

Ostroff wrote of Xerox:

> When the Xerox Corporation decided to reposition itself as "The Document Company", it concluded that it needed, in the words of chairman and chief executive Paul Allaire, "to change the basic architecture of the organisation". That meant moving away from the functional, top-down hierarchical arrangement that hindered responsiveness and accountability, and breaking into smaller market-logical pieces. The result ... is a hybrid organisation in which basic research and sales operations remain functional, while actual product design and development, manufacturing and marketing have been restructured into horizontal cross-functional business groups.

Most organisations in future will probably be hybrids, drawing the best from both the vertical and horizontal. Some organisation-wide vertical management processes, such as strategic planning, finance and human resources, will surely have to be retained in order to integrate the efforts of the horizontal operating groups. (See also The Seven Ss, page 198, and Matrix management, page 150.)

Recommended reading

Chandler, A., *Strategy and Structure: Chapters in the History of the Industrial Enterprise*, MIT Press, 1962

Chandler, A. and Deams, H. (eds), *Managerial Hierarchies: Comparative Perspectives on the Rise of Modern Industrial Enterprises*, Harvard University Press, 1980

Drucker, P., *Concept of the Corporation*, John Day, 1946

Mintzberg, H., *The Structuring of Organisations: A Synthesis of the Research*, Prentice-Hall, 1979

Mintzberg, H., *Mintzberg on Management*, The Free Press, 1989
Ostroff, F., *The Horizontal Organisation*, Oxford University Press, 1999
Weber, M., *The Theory of Social and Economic Organisation*, Free Press,
  1947

Succession planning

The idea that finding a successor to the current chief executive of an organisation is a process that should be planned and executed methodically has gathered strength in recent years. There are two types of literature on the subject.

- That which looks at ways of finding a successor to the family (or small private) business. The difficulties here are usually linked to the incumbent/founder's failure to take on board his own mortality, or his inability to tell his beloved second son that (after his death or retirement) there can be only one chief executive.
- That which looks at finding a successor to the chief executive of a large public corporation. The focus here has shifted in recent years to take in a wider constituency. Despite some writers' insistence that finding a successor is the biggest responsibility of any chief executive, no company now makes it a matter for the chief executive alone. If left to their own devices, chief executives, like anybody else, are inclined to replace themselves with a clone (on the grounds that they were without doubt the best person possible for the job).

In both cases (in the family business and the public company), there is general agreement that it is not wise to leave the choice of successor to the last minute. Any future chief executive needs to be groomed and to have a handover period when the baton of responsibility is passed from one to the other. A. Turner Foster of the Centre for Creative Leadership says:

> The ability to develop leadership in the successor generation
> is crucial to the survival and growth of family-owned and
> family-managed businesses. In order to successfully make
> the transition from one generation to the next, family
> businesses must design a process of grooming and
> developing the successor generation of the family into
> skilled leaders.

Firms increasingly turn to outside headhunters or consultants to help them choose a chief executive. These outsiders may suggest a suitable internal candidate or seek to entice an external candidate to the post. Their job is one of match-making: putting together a particular candidate's set of skills with a set of defined requirements for the post. These requirements should be different from those required by the previous chief executive since the company is bound to have moved on in the meantime.

A number of different types of successor can be identified.

- **The inside outsider.** The employee whose leadership style is completely different from that of their predecessor. This sort of appointment is made by a company in need of a drastic change in strategic direction, either because it has been passing through the doldrums or because it wants to go for growth after a period of consolidation. The classic appointment of an inside outsider was that of Sir John Harvey-Jones as chairman of ICI in 1982.
- **The outside insider.** The person who knows a lot about the company but does not actually work for it. Such a person has the objective view of the outsider without the complete ignorance that is the outsider's main drawback. Examples of outside insiders include the many management consultants who have gone on to head companies that they have advised, as well as previous employees who have spent time working elsewhere before leapfrogging back into the top post.
- **The horse-race winner.** The internal candidate who is publicly set against other internal candidates and told to compete for the job. Classic examples of this are the three-horse race set up by Walter Wriston to decide on his successor at Citicorp in 1984 (the winner was the then youthful John Reed) and the three-horse race won by Jack Welch in 1981 to find the future head of General Electric.
- **The boss's pet.** The candidate hand-picked and personally groomed by the existing chief executive over an extended period of time. When he was chairman of GE, the UK's biggest engineering company, Lord Weinstock groomed his son, Simon, to be his successor. But Simon died prematurely and the company turned to an outsider (George Simpson) to succeed Lord Weinstock.

A brief history

Until the last two decades of the 20th century, most chief executives of large companies were appointed from inside the organisation. Long experience of the company's business was considered the most important qualification. But by the end of the century many more high-flying managers were changing employer in mid-career. In 1988, on average, an executive worked for fewer than three employees in his lifetime; ten years later that average had risen to more than five.

Manfred Kets de Vries, a professor at INSEAD, an international business school near Paris, has said that the "high performers" of the late 1990s "are like frogs in a wheelbarrow; they can jump out any time". The more that high performers leap around like frogs, the more ingenious companies have to become in order to make them stay in the same wheelbarrow for long enough to reach the top.

Recommended reading

Levinson, H., "Conflicts that Plague the Family Business", *Harvard Business Review*, March-April 1971

Vancil, R.F., *Passing the Baton*, Harvard University Press, 1987

Zaleznik, A., "Managers and Leaders: Are they Different?", *Harvard Business Review*, May-June 1977

SWOT analysis

SWOT is a handy mnemonic to help planners think about corporate strategy. It stands for Strengths, Weaknesses, Opportunities and Threats. What are an organisation's SWOTs? How can it manage them in a way that will optimise its performance?

The process usually starts by listing items under the four headings; a particular strength, for example, might be a dedicated workforce or some currently valuable patents. These are then given scores according to what are seen as the main issues in the company's business environment for the next few years. If a recession is beginning and employees have to be laid off, then a dedicated workforce might be a weakness. If a boom is about to begin, however, it will be a strength.

The four features can be seen to lie along two main dimensions.

- Internal/external. The internal features are the company's own strengths and weaknesses. Analysing them is a matter of analysing the state of the company. They are things that already exist. The external features are the organisation's opportunities and the threats to its future performance. These exist only on the horizon, and they are less easy to assess and measure. They arise from things like changes in technology, demography or government policy.
- Positive/negative. The positive things are the strengths and opportunities; the negative ones are the threats and weaknesses.

SWOT analysis can be applied to many different aspects of a company's business, such as its IT capability or its knowledge (see Knowledge management, page 130). The simplicity and intuitive wholeness of the framework has helped to make it extremely popular with both corporations and governments. Nevertheless, there has been no shortage of critics. One of the main criticisms is that, in the end, SWOT analysis invariably relies on subjective judgments. Objective measures of all the ingredients in the balance simply do not exist. Some say that this does not matter, because the process of doing the analysis is more important and revealing than the results of the analysis themselves. The journey is more important than the destination.

Other critics say that:

- there is rarely any verification of the points raised;
- there is no attempt to reconcile the same elements when they are listed under different categories;
- the distinction between internal and external issues is not always clear;
- there is no process for increasing the precision of the analysis.

SWOT analysis has been used to consider not only the competitive position of different companies, but also the competitive position of different countries. An analysis of the competitive advantages and disadvantages of Germany in 1999, for example, found that the country's strengths lay in its educated and skilled workforce. Among its weaknesses were its high labour and social costs.

Recommended reading

Hill, T. and Westbrook, R., "SWOT analysis: it's time for a product recall", *Long Range Planning*, February 1997

Pickton, D.W. and Wright, S.W., "What's SWOT in strategic analysis?", *Strategic Change*, Vol. 7, No. 2, March-April 1998

Weihrich, H., "Analysing the competitive advantages and disadvantages of Germany", *European Business Review*, Vol. 99, No. 1, 1999

Synergy

What is it?

The word comes from ancient Greek. συνεργια means working together. Andrew Campbell and Michael Goold, two British academics, define it as "links between business units that result in additional value creation". It is, they go on to say, "a Holy Grail for large multi-unit companies". It is something akin to the philosopher's stone: seeming to create extra value without consuming resources.

The business gains from synergy are often not distinguished sufficiently well from those that come from combining two businesses in such a way as to create value. Synergy is passive, it happens when two things come together regardless of what else they do. If a company buys one of its major suppliers, the synergy comes from the fact that it is now a preferred customer, not from the subsequent reorganisation of the supplier's warehouses so that they are more conveniently located for their new owner.

Campbell and Goold say there are six areas where synergy can pay off in business.

- Through shared know-how.
- By co-ordinating strategies (strategy is another word that comes from ancient Greek, see page 206).
- By sharing tangible resources, such as call centres or transport fleets.
- Through vertical integration (see page 233).
- By pooling the two organisations' negotiating power, especially with suppliers. It was a key aim of the Daimler/Chrysler merger, for example, to make considerable savings in this way.
- By combining forces to create new businesses.

A brief history

Synergy has been used as part of the justification for almost every takeover since Alexander moved into Egypt. In the 20th century the idea was propagated by an anthropologist, Ruth Benedict. She used the word when writing during the second world war about communities where co-operation was rewarded and proved advantageous to all. The idea was picked up and transferred to the business world by Abraham Maslow (see Hierarchy of needs, page 113). It fitted well with Maslow's non-authoritarian model of organisational structure.

In the well-grounded conceptual framework of the value chain (see Competitive advantage, page 35), the idea of the firm as a chain of linked activities (or groups of activities), synergy has a clearly defined place. Michael Porter, for instance, has written:

> The ability to add value through competing in multiple
> businesses can be understood in terms of sharing activities
> or transferring proprietary skills across activities. This allows
> the elusive notion of synergy to be made concrete and
> rigorous.

Promises of synergy have often failed to deliver. As Campbell and Goold put it: "Synergy initiatives often fall short of management's expectations." They quote the example of a firm of consultants where, in order to gain synergy, the IT specialists were merged with the strategy specialists, until the day when the IT people found out that the strategy people were on a completely different scale of pay and perks. All the synergy gains were lost in an instant. The authors end their article by quoting the physicians' creed: "First ensure you do no harm."

Recommended reading
Goold, M. and Campbell, A., "Desperately Seeking Synergy", *Harvard Business Review*, September-October 1998

Technology transfer

How to get technology to move about – from its origins in the corporate or government laboratory to the commercial market where it can make money for its inventors and all those involved with it – has been a long-running issue for corporations and governments alike.

The transfer of technology can involve physical devices and equipment, or it can be intangible; it can involve knowledge itself or technical know-how. The transfer can take place in many different directions, from the public sector to the private sector, for example (from state universities to commercial enterprises), or from rich countries to poor countries. It can also take place in a number of different ways, via joint research projects, co-operation agreements, licensing or trade shows.

In 1992 a UN report on technology transfer declared that:

- Technology now consists of hardware (capital equipment), software (such as computer programs) and services (human skills in engineering, for example).
- Innovation now comes largely from corporations themselves, rather than academic institutions and research laboratories.
- Although much innovation originates in the multinational's home country, foreign subsidiaries and affiliates are often responsible for modifying it to suit local conditions.

Corporations export technology in various ways. For example:

- They sell new or improved products to new markets abroad. At one time the Japanese were notorious for taking new imported products to pieces in order to analyse their technology. But they were not alone.
- They take out patents in foreign countries with the aim of selling the patent or licensing the use of it. Once the patent expires, the technology that it protects comes into the public arena.
- They provide technical assistance as part of a large contract with a foreign government or firm. This type of conditional contract became increasingly common in the later years of the 20th century as developing countries saw the intensifying international competition to undertake their large public works projects. "Yes,

you can build my power station. But I want some technical expertise as part of the price."

- ◪ They make foreign direct investments (FDI). By buying a substantial stake in a foreign corporation, multinationals inject not only capital but also (to some extent) their management know-how and production skills.

Because of this activity, multinationals are crucial to any global attempt to improve the transfer of appropriate technologies to poorer countries. There are, however, considerable barriers to the transfer of technologies across borders. They include the following.

- ◪ Low local labour costs. These may discourage the application of labour-saving technologies because they radically change the balance in any cost-benefit analysis (see page 43) carried out to test the introduction of the technologies.
- ◪ A lack of local infrastructure. It is no good, for instance, introducing direct-sales techniques into a country that does not have an extensive telephone network.
- ◪ A lack of local skills or education. In particular, this means management skills. There has to be a certain level of organisational sophistication for firms to benefit from many technologies.
- ◪ Cultural and/or language barriers. Although the language of engineering is increasingly English (or, more accurately, techno-American), language is a barrier to the teaching of, say, supply chain management to Swahili speakers. Similarly, culture is a barrier to the transfer of all sorts of high-tech goods, ranging from contraceptive pills to genetically modified foods.

A brief history

The idea that the transfer of technology, either within the confines of a single country or across borders, is an important element in economic growth (and is in short supply) came late to economists. Classical theories of trade, such as those of David Ricardo, did not take account of it. In Ricardo's early 19th-century London, the dramatic impact on industrial production of inventions like the spinning jenny and the steam engine had not yet been felt.

Until the 20th century, the only factors of production that were discussed were land, labour and capital. It was not until 1966 that

Raymond Vernon, a Russian-born Harvard professor of international affairs, formally related the international spread of innovation to international trade and its cycles. Nevertheless, in the 19th century there was considerable transfer of technology across borders, particularly between the UK and the United States. Much of it occurred through the migration of people, who took their skills and technical know-how to their new country.

By the late 20th century, the main conduits of technology across borders were multinational corporations. However, there was widespread concern, both domestically and internationally, about the adequacy of flows of technology between the suppliers of it and the users of it. For example, in the United States the government fretted that research from federal laboratories was not being transferred at an acceptable rate to the market place.

One of the main reasons for this was that federal research became available to all. This was a good idea superficially, but it prevented companies from investing in it because they were then unable to protect their investment. In other words, they held back from investing in the fruits of federal laboratories because those fruits were already in the public domain. In recognition of this, the American Congress enacted several pieces of legislation in the 1980s aimed at promoting the transfer of federal technology and protecting private-sector investment in it.

Xerox is a technological innovator that has been vexed by the question of how to convert more of its own in-house inventions into money for itself rather than for those who pick them up once Xerox has discarded them. To address this problem it set up a special unit called Xerox Technology Ventures. Based in California, its job was to exploit ideas that came out of the company's research laboratories but that did not fit in with the firm's mainstream activity. When it found an idea that it wanted to transfer to the market, it took its inventors out of their comfortable laboratories, put them into cheap commercial premises, gave them a professional manager to run their business and made them the owners of up to 20% of the equity.

Recommended reading

Jeremy, D.J., *Technology Transfer and Business Enterprise*, Elgar Publishing, 1994

Vernon, R., *Sovereignty at Bay, The Multinational Spread of US Enterprises*, Basic Books, 1971

Theories X and Y

Theory X and Theory Y were devised by Douglas McGregor in his 1960 book *The Human Side of Enterprise*. They encapsulated a fundamental distinction between management styles and have formed the basis for much subsequent writing about the subject.

Theory X is the authoritarian style where the emphasis is on "productivity, on the concept of a fair day's work, on the evils of feather-bedding and restriction of output, on rewards for performance ... [it] reflects an underlying belief that management must counteract an inherent human tendency to avoid work". Theory X was the management style that predominated in business after the mechanistic systems of scientific management (see page 193) swept everything before them in the first two decades of the 20th century.

Theory Y is the participative style of management which "assumes that people will exercise self-direction and self-control in the achievement of organisational objectives to the degree that they are committed to those objectives". It is management's main job in this system to maximise that commitment.

Theory X assumes that individuals are base, work-shy and constantly in need of a good prod. It always has a ready-made excuse for failure – the innate limitations of all human resources. Theory Y, however, assumes that individuals go to work of their own accord, because work is the only way in which they have a chance of satisfying their (high-level) need for achievement and self-respect. People will work without prodding; it has been their fate since Adam and Eve were banished from the Garden of Eden. Man must work to survive.

Theory Y gives management no easy excuses for failure. It challenges them "to innovate, to discover new ways of organising and directing human effort, even though we recognise that the perfect organisation, like the perfect vacuum, is practically out of reach". McGregor urged companies to adopt Theory Y. Only it, he believed, could motivate human beings to the highest levels of achievement. Theory X merely satisfied their lower-level physical needs and could not hope to be as productive. "Man is a wanting animal," wrote McGregor, "as soon as one of his needs is satisfied, another appears in its place."

There are parallels with Abraham Maslow's hierarchy of needs (see page 113), and Maslow was indeed greatly influenced by McGregor. He tried to introduce Theory Y into a Californian electronics business, for example, but found that the idea in its extreme form did not work. All individuals, he concluded, however independent and mature, need some form of structure around them and some direction from others. Maslow also criticised Theory Y for its "inhumanity" to the weak, and to those who are not capable of a high level of self-motivation.

A brief history

Douglas McGregor died at the comparatively young age of 58 in 1964. He had a fairly straightforward academic career, lecturing at Harvard University and MIT, and becoming one of the first Sloan professors. Because of his early death he did not publish much, but what he did publish has had a great impact. In 1993 he was listed as the most popular management writer, alongside a Frenchman, Henri Fayol.

Many leading management figures who followed him, including Rosabeth Moss Kanter, Warren Bennis and Tom Peters, have acknowledged that much of modern management thinking goes back to McGregor, especially the influence of his writing on subsequent ideas about leadership.

In his comic classic *Up the Organisation*, Robert Townsend, a former president of the Avis car-hire company, wrote powerfully in support of Theory Y:

> People don't hate work. It's as natural as rest or play. They don't have to be forced or threatened. If they commit themselves to mutual objectives, they'll drive themselves more effectively than you can drive them. But they'll commit themselves only to the extent they can see ways of satisfying their ego and development needs."

Recommended reading

Lorsch, J. and Morse, J., "Beyond Theory Y", *Harvard Business Review*, May-June 1970

Maslow, A., *Eupsychian Management*, Richard D. Irwin & Dorsey Press, 1965

McGregor, D., *The Human Side of Enterprise*, McGraw Hill, 1960

McGregor, D., *Leadership and Motivation*, MIT Press, 1966

Townsend, R., *Up the Organisation*, Michael Joseph, 1970

Total quality management

Total quality management (TQM) is the idea that controlling quality is not something that is left to a "quality controller", a person who stands at the end of a production line checking final output. It is (or it should be) something that permeates an organisation from the moment its raw materials arrive to the moment its finished products leave.

TQM is a process-oriented system built on the belief that quality is simply a matter of conforming to the customer's requirements. These requirements can be measured, and deviations from them can then be prevented by means of process improvements or redesigns.

The European Foundation for Quality Management (EFQM) says that TQM strategies are characterised by the following.

- The excellence of all managerial, operational and administrative processes.
- A culture of continuous improvement in all aspects of the business.
- An understanding that quality improvement results in cost advantages and better profit potential.
- The creation of more intensive relationships with customers and suppliers.
- The involvement of all personnel.
- Market-oriented organisational practices.

Common mistakes include the following.

- Insufficient executive commitment.
- Unrealistic expectations.
- Failure to set priorities.
- Poor measurement methods.

A brief history

The idea of total quality management was developed inside a number of Japanese firms in the 1950s and 1960s. But it was built largely on the teaching of two Americans, W. Edwards Deming and J.J. Juran, who had quietly developed the principles in the aftermath of the second world war. With the help of books and articles, such as David Garvin's 1983

225

description in the *Harvard Business Review* of the way in which TQM, and other techniques practised by Japanese companies, were putting them streets ahead of their foreign competitors, the idea was later reclaimed by the United States and widely adopted by American business.

Europe, which at times looked as if it was being squeezed out of this game of American-Japanese ping-pong, also made claims to be the fount of total quality. The chairman of French car company Renault, Raymond Levy, said in the early 1990s:

> *Quality is representative of a culture which we Europeans have no reason to let others monopolise. The Europe of Descartes; the Europe of the Age of Reason and the Enlightenment; the Europe of the industrial and technological revolution of the last two centuries holds within itself all the elements of method and exactitude conveyed by the term "total quality".*

In recent years there has been some backlash against the implications of TQM, especially in the United States. Florida Power & Light, for example, the first American company to win the Deming Prize for quality management, cut its TQM programme because of its employees' complaints about the excessive amount of paperwork that it required. Douglas Aircraft, a subsidiary of McDonnell Douglas, is another company that cut its programme to next to nothing. *Newsweek* colourfully described the aircraft company's action: "At Douglas, TQM appeared to be just one more hothouse Japanese flower never meant to grow on rocky American ground."

Recommended reading

Crosby, P.B., *Quality is Free*, McGraw-Hill, 1979

Deming, W.E., *Out of the Crisis*, MIT Press, 1988

Juran. J.J. and Gryna, F.M., *Quality Control Handbook*, McGraw-Hill, 1988.

Garvin, D., "Quality on the Line", *Harvard Business Review*, September-October 1983

Hauser, J.R. and Clausing, D., "The House of Quality", *Harvard Business Review*, May-June 1988

Unbundling

The taking apart of a company, or any bundle of assets, was common practice well before the US Supreme Court decreed in 1911 that John D. Rockefeller's Standard Oil Company should be compulsorily unbundled. The court said that the company's "very genius for commercial development and organisation ... soon begat an intent and purpose to exclude others".

The degree of industrial concentration that might have come about had the unbundling of Standard Oil not occurred can be gauged from the fact that, 60 years later, one part of that company (Standard Oil of New Jersey, now called Exxon) was the third largest corporation in the world. At the same time, Standard Oil of California and Standard Oil of Indiana were the 11th and 15th largest corporations respectively.

Historically, the reasons for unbundling have fallen into two categories.

- As with Rockefeller's oil companies (and as with AT&T – Ma Bell – in the 1980s), it has been done in response to a government's wish to break up a monopoly or an undesirable degree of industrial concentration.
- It has been done for sound commercial reasons, to realise greater value through a sort of reverse synergy (see page 218) in which three minus two equals more than one. This greater value is realised either through a capital gain from the sale of the previously bundled assets (a process often referred to as asset stripping), or through an improvement in the margins on the unbundled businesses.

A brief history

Unbundling has been fashionable in phases. It generally follows an intense period of mergers and acquisitions. In the 1960s and early 1970s there was a time when asset strippers assiduously searched for quoted companies whose assets were worth more than their market value. Information about quoted companies was far less than it is today, and it was available to a far smaller number of people. As a result, it was still possible to spot genuine bargains.

Many of the asset strippers thrived on the detritus of conglomerates that had failed to produce the value that they promised. People like Jim Slater and James Goldsmith in the UK were recognised experts. James Goldsmith said that the conglomerates of the 1960s "underperformed in growth, profitability, worthwhile capital investment, creation of employment and innovation". They needed to be broken up. Jim Slater's company (Slater Walker) was a byword for asset stripping before it eventually crashed and became the subject of a Department of Trade investigation.

In the early 1990s companies again began to unbundle in a wave of enthusiasm for returning to their core competencies (see page 40) – those few things that they thought they did particularly well. This time they were not primarily concerned with asset stripping – that is, aiming to make a fast buck by buying and selling unbundled bits. They wanted to make better margins on what they chose to retain. Conglomerates again were part of the process. Companies like Hanson and BTR were 'among the bungled conglomerates that were unbundled in the 1990s. From being worth $13.4 billion at the beginning of the 1990s, Hanson's value had fallen to "only" $4.9 billion by 1997. (See also Diversification, page 66.)

Recommended reading

Hagel, J. III and Singer, M., "Unbundling the Corporation", *Harvard Business Review*, March-April 1999

Unique selling proposition

Commonly referred to as a USP, a unique selling proposition is a description of the qualities that are unique to a particular product or service and that differentiate it in a way which will make customers purchase it rather than its rivals.

Marketing experts used to insist that every product and service had to have a USP, at least one unique feature that could be distilled into a 60-second sales spiel, the equivalent of a single written paragraph. But this idea was usurped by the view that what really matters in marketing a product or service is its positioning, where it sits on the spectrum of customer needs. Shampoos, for instance, claim to meet all sorts of different customer needs and sit in all sorts of different positions – the need to wash dry hair or greasy hair, dark hair or blond hair, or the need to wash hair frequently or not so frequently. Few of them, however, can claim to have a unique selling proposition.

Uniqueness is rare, and coming up with a continuous stream of products with unique features is, in practice, extremely difficult. Philip Kotler says that the difficulty firms have in creating functional uniqueness has made them "focus on having a unique emotional selling proposition (an ESP) instead of a USP". He gives the example of the Ferrari car and the Rolex watch. Neither has a distinctive functional uniqueness, but each has a unique emotional association in the consumer's mind.

Uniqueness can be achieved in various ways.

- By offering the lowest price. A British department store, John Lewis, claims that it is "never knowingly undersold". Its USP establishes it as the cheapest vendor (under certain prescribed conditions) of the items that it sells. This is a rocky route to success, however, particularly at a time when there are firms prepared to sell (temporarily) at below cost just to establish turnover. This was the case with many of the early Internet retailing experiments. Moreover, buyers who base their purchasing decisions on price alone are often disloyal. Customers continue to go to John Lewis for many reasons other than its price promise.
- By offering the highest quality. This is the Rolls-Royce approach to selling.
- By being exclusive. In the information age, this is an increasingly

common type of USP. More and more firms offer a unique packaging of information or knowledge.

■ By offering the best customer service. Domino's Pizza became the best-selling brand in the United States on the basis of its USP: "Fresh, hot pizza delivered in 30 minutes or less, guaranteed." It did not promise high quality or low price, just fast delivery. A side benefit of a USP like this is that it compels the firm's employees to try that bit harder to achieve the promise. A firm that fails to fulfil the promise of its USP, however, is condemned to bankruptcy if it does not quickly come up with a new one.

■ By offering the widest choice. This is particularly appropriate to niche markets. A specialist cheese shop, say, can claim to offer a wider selection of cheeses than anyone else.

■ By giving the best guarantee. This is particularly important in certain industries, such as the travel trade and catalogue selling, where customers pay for something upfront and then have to hope that what they think they have bought is eventually delivered.

Jay Abraham, a marketing consultant who describes himself as "the most expensive and successful marketing consultant on the planet", says that most businesses do not have a USP:

> [They have] only a "me too", rudderless, nondescript, unappealing business that feeds solely upon the sheer momentum of the marketplace. There's nothing unique; there's nothing distinct. They promise no great value, benefit, or service – just "buy from us" for no justifiable, rational reason.

Recommended reading
www.abraham.com/articles

Value chain

The idea of the value chain first appeared in the second chapter of Michael Porter's book, *Competitive Advantage, Creating and Sustaining Superior Performance*. In it he wrote:

> A systematic way of examining all the activities a firm
> performs and how they interact is necessary for analysing
> the sources of competitive advantage [see page 35]. In this
> chapter, I introduce the value chain as the basic tool for
> doing so.

In the decade after the book was first published (in 1985) the idea became one of the most discussed and most misunderstood in the whole of the management arena.

Each link in a value chain consists of a bundle of activities (value activities), and these bundles are performed by a firm to "design, produce, market, deliver and support its product". "Value activities are the discrete building blocks of competitive advantage," wrote Porter.

Rival firms may have similar chains, but they may also differ greatly. Porter quoted the example of People Express, one of the earliest of the low-cost airlines, and United Airlines, a traditional player in the industry. They were both in the same business, but there were significant differences in the way that, for example, they ran their boarding gate operations, their aircraft operations and their crews. Differences such as these, claimed Porter, are a principal source of competitive advantage.

Critics of the idea focused on the difficulty in identifying the discrete building blocks. Without defining them carefully it is not possible to compare and contrast them with those of rivals and thereby to gain competitive advantage. Porter tried to help. He said:

> [Every value activity] employs purchased inputs, human
> resources (labour and management), and some form of
> technology to perform its function. Each value activity also
> uses and creates information ... the appropriate degree of
> disaggregation depends on the economics of the activities
> and the purposes for which the value chain is being
> analysed.

He also said a bit about what value chains were not. For instance: "Value activities and accounting classifications are rarely the same," he explained. But still, firms found it hard to spot a value activity when it hit them on the factory floor. Non-manufacturing businesses found it even harder.

A brief history

Since Porter introduced the idea of the value chain, the concept has been taken in a number of different directions. One has attempted to extend it beyond the straightforward manufacturing processes for which it was, in its early form, most suited. Richard Norman and Rafael Ramirez argued that the value chain was outdated, suited to a slower changing world of comparatively fixed markets. Companies in the 1990s, they said, needed not just to add value but to "reinvent" it. This they could do by reconfiguring roles and relationships between "a constellation of actors" – suppliers, partners, customers, and so on. One company they pointed to as having done this successfully was IKEA, a Swedish-based international retailer of home furniture.

Jeffrey Rayport and John Sviokla applied the idea to the virtual world, the world of information, arguing that managers must pay attention to the way in which companies create value in both the tangible world of the market place and the virtual world of the market space. Just as companies take raw materials and refine them into products, so (increasingly) do they take raw information and add value to it. This, say Rayport and Sviokla, they achieve through a sequence of five activities: information gathering, organising, selecting, synthesising and distributing.

Recommended reading

Egan, G., *Adding Value*, Jossey-Bass, 1993

Freeman, E. and Liedtka, J., "Stakeholder Capitalism and the Value Chain", *European Management Journal*, June 1997

Norman, R. and Ramirez, R., "From Value Chain to Value Constellation: Designing Interactive Strategy", *Harvard Business Review*, January-February 1993

Porter, M., *Competitive Advantage, Creating and Sustaining Superior Performance*, Free Press, 1985

Rayport, J.F. and Sviokla, J.J., "Exploiting the Virtual Value Chain", *Harvard Business Review*, January-February 1995

Vertical integration

Vertical integration is the merging together of two businesses that are at different levels of production, such as a food manufacturer with a chain of supermarkets. Merging in this way with something further down the production process (and thus closer to the final consumer) is known as forward integration. Merging with something further back in the process (such as a food manufacturer merging with a farm) is known as backward integration. Businesses are downstream or upstream of each other depending on whether they are nearer to or further away from the final consumer (the sea to which the river of production flows).

Vertical integration is to be distinguished from horizontal integration, which is the merging together of businesses that are at the same level of production, such as two supermarkets, or two food manufacturers. The integration of two organisations that are in completely different lines of business is sometimes referred to as conglomerate integration (see also Diversification, page 66).

The benefits of vertical integration come from an organisation's greater ability to control access to inputs and to control the cost, quality and delivery times of these inputs. In line with the fading popularity of the command-and-control type of organisational structure in the late 20th century, however, this logic became less compelling.

In the late 1990s consultants McKinsey & Co wrote:

> Whereas historically firms have vertically integrated in
> order to control access to scarce physical resources, modern
> firms are internally and externally disaggregated,
> participating in a variety of alliances and joint ventures
> and outsourcing even those activities normally regarded as
> core.

Note that the word for the opposite of integrated is disaggregated, not, as it sometimes appears it should be, disintegrated.

Vertical integration has been a difficult strategy for companies to implement successfully. It is often complex, expensive and hard to reverse. Upstream producers frequently integrate with downstream distributors to secure a market for their output. This is fine when times are good. But many firms have found themselves cutting prices sharply to their downstream distributors when demand has fallen just to maintain their level of plant utilisation. This has often had the effect of driving non-integrated competitors out of the business, and leaving customers highly resistant to any subsequent price increase.

The vertically integrated giants of the computer industry, such as IBM, Digital and Burroughs, were felled like young saplings when Apple got together with Intel and Microsoft at the end of the 1970s and formed a network of independent specialists that produced machines far more efficiently than the do-it-all giants.

A brief history

Some of the most visible examples of vertical integration have taken place in the oil industry. In the 1970s and 1980s many companies that were primarily engaged in exploration and the extraction of crude petroleum decided to acquire downstream refineries and distribution networks. Companies such as Shell and BP controlled and owned every single process involved in bringing a drop of oil from their North Sea or Alaskan origins to a car's petrol tank.

The idea of vertical integration was taken a step further by Dell Computer, one of the most successful companies of the 1990s. Its founder, Michael Dell, said that he combined the traditional vertical integration of the supply chain with the special characteristics of the virtual organisation to create what he calls "virtual integration". Dell assembles computers from other firms' parts, but it has relationships with these firms that are more binding than those of the traditional buyer/supplier. It does not own them in the way of the vertically integrated firm, but through the use of information and a variety of loose associations it achieves the same aim: "a tightly co-ordinated supply chain".

Recommended reading

Dell, M., Magretta, J. and Rollins, K., "The power of virtual integration: an interview with Dell Computer's Michael Dell", *Harvard Business Review*, March-April 1998

Stuckey, J. and White, D., "When and When Not to Vertically Integrate", *McKinsey Quarterly*, No. 3, 1993

The virtual organisation

Although it is widely alleged that the business organisation of the future will be virtual, precise definitions of the phrase are hard to find among those who make the allegation. But its origin is clear. It lies in the expression virtual reality, an experience in which electronically created sounds and images are made to resemble reality. A virtual company resembles a normal traditional company in its inputs and its outputs. It differs in the way in which it adds value during the journey in between.

A virtual organisation is easy to recognise. One of the most celebrated is the UK's Virgin Group. In 1995 it took 5% of the British cola market with just five employees. This was achieved by tightly focusing on the company's core competence (see page 40), namely, its marketing. Everything else, from the production of the drink to the distribution of it, was done by somebody else.

In his book *Destination Z*, Robert Baldock says that becoming virtual involves "the removal of constraints of time, place and form ... made possible by the convergence of computing, telecommunications and visual media". The virtual organisation has an almost infinite variety of structures, all of them fluid and changing. Most of them, like Virgin, need virtually no employees. One New York insurance company was started from scratch by someone whose overriding aim was to employ nobody but himself.

The virtual organisation de-emphasises the importance of physical assets. This reflects the fact that adding value is becoming more dependent on (mobile) knowledge and less dependent on (immobile) physical assets. A virtual organisation also has few full-time staff of its own, relying for the most part on a network of part-time electronically connected freelancers, sometimes referred to as e-lancers.

Linked to the idea of the virtual organisation is the idea of the virtual office, a place where space is not allocated uniquely to individual employees. People work as and when they need to, wherever space is available. This practice is commonly referred to as hot desking. The virtual office has the advantage of providing a different vista every day. But it makes it difficult to form close relationships with colleagues.

In *Rethinking the Future*, Lester Thurow, a former dean of the Sloan School of Management, gave a vivid portrayal of the virtual office:

*You walk in and there's an electronic board that says room
1021 is empty. You go to 1021. You have your personal
telephone number. You call up your computer code. You
press a button and your family picture is up on the flat-
screen TV set on the wall. And that's your office for as long
as you're there. The minute you leave, it ceases to be your
office.*

*We know why you don't do that at the moment; human
beings like to have a cave. But the first company that figures
out how to make this work will save 25% on office space,
25% on telephones, 25% on computers. These will be the low-
cost producers, and low-cost producers will inherit the
earth.*

An American telecoms company, AT&T, reckons that it saved over
$500m between 1991 and 1998 by reorganising its office space along
virtual lines.

A brief history

The process of becoming a virtual organisation is a gradual one that takes
place over a period of time. As companies withdraw more and more into
their core competencies, so they become more virtual. The virtual organisation is able to leverage this core into almost any industrial sector.
Thus it can be in the pensions business and the railway business at the
same time (as is the Virgin organisation in the UK). It can then rapidly
desert any one of these businesses, and equally rapidly move into
something completely different by means of strategic alliances with
organisations that have the essential skills that it lacks. It can do this
anywhere in the world.

Hollywood is often quoted as the template for the virtual organisation.
The way that movies have been made ever since the industry freed itself
from the old studio system (where everybody from Cary Grant down to
the doorman was a full-time employee) has been virtual. A number of
freelancers, from actors to directors via set builders and publicity agents,
come together with a common purpose: to make a movie, to tell a story
on celluloid. They then go their separate ways and another (unrelated)
bunch of people (with a similar set of skills) comes together to make
another movie. And so it goes on, very productively.

The virtual organisation is more ephemeral than corporations of the
past. It is more difficult to define its corporate history because it has no

repository of long-term memory, the individual who has worked for the same organisation for the best part of half a century. Nor has it any long-term geographical presence or a local community that remembers "Old Mr Chambers from way back".

Recommended reading

Baldock, R., *Destination Z*, John Wiley, 1999

Davidow, W.H. and Malone, M.S., *The Virtual Corporation*, Harper Business, 1992

Hamel, G. and Prahalad, C.K., *Competing for the Future*, HBR Press, 1994

Handy, C., "Trust and the Virtual Organisation", *Harvard Business Review*, May-June 1995

Malone, T.W. and Laubacher, R.J., "The Dawn of the E-lance Economy", *Harvard Business Review*, September-October 1998

Thurow, L., *Rethinking the Future*, Nicholas Brealey, 1997

Vision

A vision is the image that a business must have of its goals before it sets out to reach them. It is a bit like the old saying: "If you don't know where you're going, then sure as anything you won't get there." Warren Bennis, a noted writer on leadership, says:

> To choose a direction, an executive must first have developed a mental image of the possible and desirable future state of the organisation. This image, which we call a vision, may be as vague as a dream or as precise as a goal or a mission statement.

In the early 1960s, John Kennedy had a vision of putting a man on the moon by 1970; in the 1980s, Sanford Weill had a vision of making American Express the leading investment bank within five years. IBM's vision at the time was even vaguer: to provide the best service of any firm in the world.

Great leaders create great visions. In *Dynamic Administration*, an American political scientist, Mary Parker Follett, wrote: "The most successful leader of all is the one who sees another picture not yet actualised. He sees the things which belong in his present picture but which are not yet there." Peter Drucker has argued that corporate success depends on the vision articulated by the chief executive.

This description of Napoleon is from his contemporary biographer, Louis Madelin:

> He would deal with three or four alternatives at the same time and endeavour to conjure up every possible eventuality – preferably the worst. This foresight, the fruit of meditation, generally enabled him to be ready for any setback, nothing ever took him by surprise ... perhaps the most astonishing characteristic of his intellect was the combination of idealism and realism which enabled him to face the most exalted visions at the same time as the most insignificant realities. And, indeed, he was in a sense a visionary, a dreamer of dreams.

For a vision to have any impact on the employees of an organisation it has to be conveyed in a dramatic and enduring way. Metaphor is often useful: "a chicken in every pot" is the standard off-the-shelf vision for the politician promising a programme of rapid economic improvement. Jan Carlzon, the legendary leader of Scandinavian Airline Systems (SAS) in the 1980s, once outlined his vision for the "Passenger Pleasing Plane". With seating never more than two abreast and higher roofs, Carlzon said that his starting point was: "An aircraft which the passenger wants. Then we can add on engines and the cockpit, not the other way around." Unfortunately, Carlzon did not survive in the industry long enough to turn his particular vision into reality.

A brief history

James Collins and Jerry Porras were largely responsible for a revival of interest in the "visioning thing" in the mid-1990s with their best-selling book *Built to Last*. It related corporate longevity to a company's vision and to its goals. The average age of the authors' sample of enduringly successful companies was 97. They wrote:

> The lessons of these companies can be learned and applied by the vast majority of managers at all levels. Gone forever – at least in our eyes – is the debilitating perspective that the trajectory of a company depends on whether it is led by people ordained with rare and mysterious qualities that cannot be learned by others.

And with that, a large number of managers who knew that they were not ordained with rare and mysterious qualities rushed out and bought the book.

The authors have been criticised for the fact that 17 out of the 18 companies they examined were American. (The one outsider was Sony.) Experience of corporate longevity is undoubtedly greater in Europe and Japan than it is in the United States. It would have been interesting to look at experience there with the visioning thing.

Recommended reading

Collins, J.C. and Porras, J.I., *Built to Last, Successful Habits of Visionary Companies*, Random House, 1994
Collins, J.C. and Porras, J.I., "Building Your Company's Vision", *Harvard Business Review*, September-October 1996

Zero-base budgeting

Once upon a time a business's annual budget was drawn up on the basis of the previous year's budget. To each item that appeared last year, managers would add a certain percentage. The percentage would be determined more or less arbitrarily, although it would probably be related in some indeterminate way to the rate of inflation, the company's overall strategy and the manager's frame of mind that day.

For many years it was widely recognised that this was not an ideal way to allocate a company's scarce financial resources. It encouraged managers to focus on the cost increases from year to year rather than on the underlying costs themselves. It also inadequately took account of the rapidly changing environment in which a company operated. For example, increasing last year's expenditure on IT by the rate of inflation "plus some" was, at some stage, sure to leave a business way behind its rivals.

Nobody came up with something better until Peter Pyhrr, a manager at the Texas Instrument company in Dallas, developed the idea of zero-base budgeting. Each year he prepared his budgets as if last year's figures had not existed. Every assumption had to be rethought from scratch and then justified. It was not acceptable to use last year's expenditure as a benchmark for this year's budgeted costs, and then only to have to justify the increase on that expenditure. In effect, zero-base budgeting treats all claims on financial resources as if they were entirely new claims for entirely new projects.

A basic requirement of zero-base budgeting is that managers prepare budgets for the cost of running their operations at a minimum level. They are then required to calculate the costs and benefits of making a particular business decision which would lead to an incremental increase from that level. Breaking the budget down into different decision packages in this way makes it easier for senior managers to make choices among competing claims on scarce resources.

The idea was rapidly adopted by other companies. It has also been used extensively by local and national governments and by health and education authorities, areas where the budgeting process has traditionally rolled over from one year to the next with its underlying assumptions rarely questioned.

Criticism of zero-base budgeting focuses on the practical difficulties of implementation, and on the fact that this makes it time-consuming. Traditional incremental budgeting retains the great advantage of simplicity. Another author claims that "recent history has indicated that zero-base budgeting is very susceptible to political influence and pressures".

Recommended reading

Pyhrr, P., *Zero-base Budgeting: a Practical Management Tool for Evaluating Expenses*, John Wiley, 1978